To David,
A fine typographer,
A fine art director,
A fine fellow.

Best wishes.

Marc x

Designer: John O'Driscoll.
The advertisements have been reproduced with the kind permission of Doyle Dane Bernbach Inc. USA, Volkswagen (GB) Limited, Volkswagenwerk A.G. and Volkswagen of America.
The US New Beetle ads appear with the kind permission of Arnold Communications.

Printed in Holland by PlantijnCasparie. Paper 135 gsm. Headline typeface: Futura Demi Bold. Body text: Futura Light.
Published by Enterprise Millenium International Ltd, 211-212 Piccadilly, London, W1V 9LD. Telephone +44 20 7830 9692
 First published 1982. Reprint 1993. This edition published October 2000.

ISBN 0 9537032 1 5

This third edition is dedicated to the
late Helmut Krone.

Our thanks to the following, without whom this book would not have seen the light of day.

Roger Baker. Claes Bergquist. John Borkett. David Brown. Tony Byrne. Martin Carey. David Cheetham. Ed Church. Roy Dina. Lucky Dissanyake. Face Type Limited. Brian Fowler. Paul Garrett. Herr H.E. Hassemer. Brian Hill. Steve Hobbs. Henri Holmgren. David Horry. Jigsaw Artists. Ron Lawner. Graham Lincoln. Emma Lincoln. John Londei. Richard Mummery. Lars Ohlsson. Peter Owen Peter Pleasance. Terry Potts. John Slaven. Studio 10. David Taylor. Vanessa Volger. Gary Whipps. John Withers. Mike Wright

Our thanks also to Volkworld Magazine for their support in the preparation of this third edition.

Contents

Introduction.   Page   7

About the car.   Page   9

About the campaign.   Page   12

Beetle advertising.   Page   16

Nine ways to improve an ad.   Page 112

Station Wagon advertising.   Page 117

Karmann Ghia advertising.   Page 157

Fastback, Squareback and 411 advertising.   Page 171

VW advertising outside the USA.   Page 185

New Beetle advertising.   Page 217

When we first decided to put this book together, some twenty years ago, we knew it was going to be a labour of love.

We'd all owned Beetles in our day and we'd all been involved in Volkswagen advertising. One of us as a client, one as an art director and one as a copywriter.

To let the Beetle and its advertising pass on without a permanent record seemed a crying shame.

For surely, no car was ever more loved, no car advertising more admired.

This book is the story of the car and its advertising. In a unique way the two were indivisible; the charming honest advertising became part of the charm and honesty of the car.

If you ever owned a Beetle, if you've ever chuckled at a Volkswagen advertisement, or if you simply appreciate wit and style, you'll enjoy this book.

To Volkswagen who made the car and to Doyle Dane Bernbach who made the ads, must go all the credit.

We have simply been willing editors.

Alfredo Marcantonio.

John O'Driscoll

David Abbott.

About the car.

No book about Volkswagen advertising would be complete without some reference to the car's early history and some tribute to the man who designed it, Ferdinand Porsche.

Although a student of electrical engineering, Porsche turned his attention to the horseless carriage early in his career, producing a revolutionary hub transmission system for electric cars at the age of twenty-five. A design that won him the Grand Prix at the Paris exposition of 1900.

Within six years he had become technical director of the Austro Daimler Car Company.

There followed a string of top jobs within Germany's prospering auto industry, ending with Porsche forming his own independent design "Buro" early in the 1930's.

During this period Porsche emerged as probably the greatest auto engineer of his time.

He was responsible for a whole string of ingenious yet successful designs, including the classic Mercedes SS sports models and the remarkable 16-cylinder, 250 miles per hour, Auto Union racing car that brought Germany a clutch of Grand Prix victories in the mid-thirties.

Despite his association with these exotic machines, Porsche fostered the idea of producing a people's car. He had interested several potential manufacturers in the project, but had never been able to develop it very far.

The concept of a people's car was in Hitler's mind too and eventually a meeting was arranged so that the designer could outline his plans to the German leader.

Hitler was impressed enough with what he heard to offer to pay for the development of the car.

And Porsche began work in earnest.

The vehicle that he set about building was unlike its contemporaries in almost every respect.

The engine was cooled not with water, but by air, so it would not boil of freeze. It was mounted over the back wheels to improve traction and eliminate the need for a drive shaft.

The wheels were each sprung independently, using torsion bars instead of bulkly leaf springs, saving weight and space.

And, most revolutionary of all, in place of a girder frame there was a corrugated floorpan chassis that harnessed the rigidity of the bodyshell.

Hitler re-named the Volkswagen the "Strength through joy car" or Kdf wagen.

He also instituted a special savings stamp scheme. This generated some of the funds needed to build the VW factory and enabled the poorly paid German working man to save steadily for a car of his own.

Thousands of Germans saved millions of Marks for their VWs but by the outbreak of war not one car had been produced.

Between 1939 and 1945 the newly constructed factory in Wolfsburg was turned over to the production of the VW based Kubelwagen jeep and small heating stoves for use by the troops on the Russian front.

At the end of the war the British Army put Major Ivan Hurst in charge of the bombed out Wolfsburg plant. Starved of raw materiels he set up a string of ingenious barter deals that enabled production of the Beetle to be started for the very first time.

Anxious to capitalise on his efforts, the Army offered the factory to a number of British car makers as a going concern.

As examples of short-sightedness, their reactions must rank alongside Chamberlain's famous speech after Munich.

Earnest Breech of the Ford Motor Company reported back to his US headquarters: "Mr Ford, I don't think what we are being offered here is worth a damn."

Lord Rootes head of the 1946 British trade commission was equally unimpressed. "A car like this will remain popular for two or three years if that. To build the car commercially would be a completely uneconomic enterprise."

The man who proved these experts wrong was Heinz Nordhoff, a Detroit trained ex-director of General Motor's Opel subsidiary and the man the British Army put in charge of the factory early in 1948.

Under his leadership production and sales at Wolfsburg rose steadily. Just 6,000 cars were produced in 1947 but 19,000 were built in1948. 46,000 in 1949. And 90,000 in1950.

By 1960, 865,000 cars were being produced annually.

And during 1968, the year Nordhoff died, the number of VW's being built topped 1.6 million.

The Beetle was well on its way to overtaking the Model T Ford as the world's most produced car.

During his years in power, Heinz Nordhoff decided to extend Porche's basic concept by introducing several other rear-engined, air cooled models.

But within five years of his departure this range was being phased out and the company introduced a new generation of Volkswagens. Most notably the Golf. These were advanced cars with water-cooled engines and front wheel drive.

They proved so successful in both Europe and the USA that on the evening of January 19th 1978, the unthinkable happened.

Beetle production in Germany stopped.

Although the car was declared commercially dead in Europe it refuses to lie down.

It has not been advertised of promoted for more than 20 years, yet cars continue to imported on a regular basis, from VW factories as far away as Mexico and Brazil.

About the campaign.

The Volkswagen Beetle was far from unknown in the United States when Doyle Dane Bernbach was awarded the VW advertising account in 1959.

A steady stream of VW's had been reaching the States ever since the end of the Second World War and during the mid-fifties this had swollen to a torrent.

In 1953, after a couple of unsuccessful attempts to market their car in the USA, VW managed to establish a strong network of Distributors and Dealers.

The effect on the company's sales was dramatic.

Just over 2,000 VW's were sold in the States during 1953. But by 1958, sales had topped the the 150,000 mark.

This change of fortunes is even more remarkable when you realise just how odd those early Beetles must have appeared to American eyes.

At least other European imports of the day had bonnets and boots, small though they may be. The Beetle was so rounded front and rear it was hard to tell if it was coming or going. As one wit said at the time "it looked like a motorised tortoise."

But by the early fifties the Beetle looked increasingly attractive to the growing numbers of US drivers who were sick of the big car diet dished up by Detroit: vast, thirsty machines that sprouted changes annually for obsolescence's sake.

This disenchanted minority gave Europe's car makers a first foothold in the huge US car market.

And with it the dollar almighty on exchange markets they were quick to take advantage of it.

Sadly, many of those early imports weren't fully suited to operation in the States and they proved unreliable on long runs and in very hot or cold weather.

In contrast, the Beetle with its simple air-cooled engine, quickly earned a reputation for being a "tireless performer" that was utterly reliable.

The Beetle's success in the mid-fifties was achieved without advertising, but early in 1959, despite a 5 months' waiting list for cars, VW decided to appoint an advertising agency.

The man behind the decision was Carl Hahn.

That Autumn Detroit's big three, Ford, GM and Chrysler were to introduce compact cars in an attempt to stem the growing flood of foreign machines that were reaching the USA.

Hahn had recently arrived from Germany charged with the task of resisting this counter-attack.

He was confident that advertising would help VW weather the coming storm. He also expected that at 160,000 per year the company's sales were close to the maximum that could be achieved on owner recommendation and dealer promotion alone.

Finding a suitable advertising agency proved more difficult than he at first thought.

It took him three months. And according to his own estimate, involved him in meeting more than 4,000 American admen.

Hahn was far from impressed with what he saw.

It was hardly surprising. At the time the US advertising industry was infatuated with research, think tanks, brainstorming sessions and the like.

Ads, commercials and posters were tested before they ran, while they ran and after they ran.

And the findings deeply analysed in an attempt to make the sales message mean all things to all men.

More often than not, the work that resulted ended up meaning nothing to anyone. Except of course, the agency and the client involved.

Car advertising was one of the worst offenders.

Hahn's fortuitous meeting with DDB came about via a VW distributor, Arthur Stanton.

Stanton, impressed by the work that DDB had done for Ohrbachs, the New York fashion store, had asked the agency to do some ads for the launch of his new VW Distributorship.

He was pleased enough with the work they did to give a favourable report on the agency to Carl Hahn and recommend that he saw them.

In contrast to most of the companies that Hahn had visited, DDB didn't show speculative creative work for the Beetle. They simply presented the work they were doing for their existing clients.

DDB had been formed just ten years earlier, when Bill Bernbach and Ned Doyle left Grey Advertising and joined the small ad agency run by their mutual friend, Mac Dane.

The new agency quickly earned a reputation for unusual, effective advertising by producing some highly creative work for clients like Ohrbachs, El Al, Polaroid and Levy's Rye bread.

Hahn was impressed by the agency's integrity, as well as its track record, and awarded the agency the Beetle account.

The smaller commercial vehicles business went to Fuller, Smith and Ross, an agency that specialised in industrial advertising.

The first creative team to work on the account at DDB was art director Helmut Krone and copywriter Julian Koenig.

It proved to be an inspired choice.

Together with Bill Bernbach, these two men created a look and tone of voice totally unheard of in car advertising.

Realistic photographs without flattering airbrush work or lens distortion replaced the fanciful illustrations that were 'de-rigeur' in car ads at the time.

There was no mansion or stable behind the car. No suave, debonair driver. And no admiring female.

The copy talked to the reader as though he were a close friend, not some distant moron, and was self-deprecating rather than self-congratulatory.

The overall impression given was one of friendly straight-forwardness and disarming honesty.

It's hard to imagine just how those first VW ads must have looked to the casual reader of a 1959 New Yorker magazine. One thing is for sure, they worked.

No sooner had the campaign started than advertising industry researchers found the ads were getting unusually high readership scores.

Within a year the campaign had become a conversation piece. The acid test, whether or not the ads were selling cars, came when Detroit's compacts were launched.

Within 24 months of these small cars being launched by Ford, GM and Chrysler, imported car sales in the US plummeted. From a high of 614,131 in 1960 they fell to 339,160 in 1962.

Unbelievably, VW sales were unaffected.

In fact they rose, reaching 200,000 in 1962.

Those extra sales were obviously not due solely to DDB's campaign. But it is clear that the advertising did help.

VW dealers often found that customers arrived in their showrooms with the headline of the latest DDB ad on their lips.

The final seal was set on the VW and DDB marriage in 1960 when, finding that the two agency arrangement wasn't really working out, VW moved all its advertising business to DDB.

Even with such successful advertising and an obviously good personal relationship between agency and client, not every ad that DDB presented was approved by VW.

But if you're hoping to see any of those turned-down ads or any of the dozen of others that didn't run, you're going to be disappointed.

The ads, posters and commercials that did see the light of day represent more great advertising than we have room for.

What you see on the following pages represents just a part of the iceberg of great creative work that DDB have produced on the Volkswagen account.

We hope you agree that it's the tip.

©1959 Volkswagen

Who

The Jones drive a Volkswagen and
wagens look alike from year to year.

A Volkswagen is never outmoded. In
no one knows how long a Volkswagen
the first VWs made have not worn out

'ear car do the Jones drive?

from VW owners who have clocked 100,000 miles without engine repair (if ever should need it, they will find VW ce is as good as the car).

e Volkswagen does change — where it

counts. An anti-sway bar has just been added to the front suspension to make curves even smoother. New insulation deadens engine and roadway noise.

Over the years almost every part in the

Volkswagen has been changed (but not its heart or face).

 Volkswagen owners find this a happy way to drive — and to live. How about you?

Can you name this car?

Clue: Even on the hottest day, you won't see this car with its hood up. (The engine is cooled by air instead of water. Won't overheat, won't freeze.)

Clue: It cruises at 70 miles an hour all day long without working up a sweat or running up a repair bill.

Clue: In mud, sand, ice or snow, where other cars skid, this one will go. (The engine in the rear does it.)

Clue: It's put together so air-tight, there have been persistent reports it will even float.

Clue: It's never been changed for the sake of change—and it won't be, either.

Clue: It sells for $1,565,* complete with body. And a used one depreciates less than any other car.

Clue: Its initials are VW.

The only water a Volkswagen needs is the water you wash it with.

All car engines must be cooled. But how? Conventional cars are cooled by water. The Volkswagen engine is cooled by air.

The advantages are astonishing, when you think about it. Your Volkswagen cannot boil over in summer or freeze in winter, since air neither boils nor freezes.

You need no anti-freeze. You have no radiator problems. In fact, you have no radiator. In midsummer traffic jams, your VW can idle indefinitely, while other cars and tempers boil.

The doughty Volkswagen engine is unique in still other ways. Its location in the rear means better traction (in mud, sand, ice, snow, where

other cars skid, you go). And since it is cast of aluminum-magnesium alloys, you save weight and increase efficiency. Your VW delivers an honest 32 miles to the gallon, regular driving, regular gas. And you will probably never need oil between changes.

Dale Tuttle, Manager of Sea Imports, Sioux Falls, S.D., presides over 5,008 VW parts.

Repair 'em? I've got enough parts to build 'em!

There are 5,008 parts in a Volkswagen sedan and Dale Tuttle has all of them in stock or on tap. (So does every other authorized Volkswagen dealer.)

You don't wait to get a Volkswagen serviced. Mr. Tuttle repairs even vintage VWs with equal facility; their heart and face have remained the same.

Volkswagen parts are inexpensive. A new front fender is $21.75.* A cylinder head is only $19.95.*

Volkswagen service is fast (an engine can be removed and replaced in 90 minutes!)

If you lived in Bangalore, India, and ordered a Volkswagen we wouldn't deliver it. No VW service nearby.

VW spare parts are taken from regular production, identical with those in the car itself, and so just as good. The intriguing thing is, they are seldom needed.

Why so many Volkswagens live to be 100,000.

The Volkswagen isn't the kind of a car you trade in after a year or two.

It's designed and built for keeps.

The pistons in a VW travel a shorter distance per mile than almost any other car in the world. That means less wear. Engine friction and stress are so low that cruising speed is the same as top speed!

Continuity in making the same basic model year after year has led to Volkswagen's quality of assembly—the kind that a 55,000 car would be proud of; to say nothing of a car that sells for $1,565.*

Just to give you an idea: A Volkswagen is so airtight, it's a good practice to open the window before you slam the door. Even

after you've had it for several years.

So. If you own a '56 or '57 VW that you've taken good care of, why wouldn't you want to trade it in for a '61—which looks just like it?

You wouldn't.

You'd keep it, and have the pleasure of seeing 99,999 on your VW's odometer turn to xxxxx.

© 1960 VOLKSWAGEN

The famous Italian designer suggested one change.

Just because the appearance of the Volkswagen doesn't change from year to year, don't think we take it for granted.

Some time ago, we called in a world-famous Italian body designer and we asked him what changes he would recommend in the design of the Volkswagen.

He studied it and studied it. Then he said, "Make the rear window larger."

"That's all?"

"That's all."

We did, starting with the '58 VW.

The Volkswagen is never changed to make it different. Only to make it better.

Changes take place throughout the year. 19 functional improvements have been made in the 1960 VW so far; improvements in handling, in ride, in durability. But your eye wouldn't detect these changes unless we pointed them out. A nice Volkswagen touch is that most of the new parts are interchangeable; they can also be used on previous-year VWs.

 We think the Volkswagen approach to automobile design makes sense. It might even turn out to be the most advanced styling idea of all.

We've gone places!

Ten years ago, the first Volkswagens were imported into the U.S.A.

These strange little cars with their beetle shape were almost unknown.

All they had to recommend them was 32 miles to the gallon (regular gas, regular driving), an aluminum air-cooled rear engine that could go 70 mph all day long without strain,

a sensible size for a family, and a sensible price-tag too.

Beetles multiply, so do Volkswagens. By 1954, VW was the best-selling imported car in America. It has held that rank each year since. In 1959 over 150,000 Volkswagens were sold, including station wagons and trucks.

Millionaires buy them, so do working peo-

ple and college kids. Their snub noses are familiar in every state of the Union, as American as apple strudel.

Volkswagen is an honest car. We put as much as we can into it, and we think it's the best car in the world for your money. We're glad so many other people agree.

It isn't so.

That winding key you've been seeing lately on some Volkswagens is not standard equipment.

It's put there by proud VW owners, who go around telling their friends they get 40 miles on one winding.

That isn't quite true.

The correct figure is about 32 miles (regular driving), and it requires one gallon of gas.

Otherwise, the winder gives you a

pretty good idea of how economical it is to keep up a VW.

The Volkswagen engine in the rear is air-cooled. No water to boil over in the summer. No water to freeze in the winter. No anti-freeze. No radiator expenses. No radiator, period.

Engine friction is so low that top speed and cruising speed are one and the same. A Volkswagen can run wide-open all day long without running up a repair

bill. And it uses practically no oil between changes.

A Volkswagen costs $0,000, including heater and defroster. Leatherette upholstery is optional, and so are white wall tires, a side view mirror and radio. Outside of that, we can't think of anything else you might want.

Except possibly that winding key.

Come in today and take a turn . . . in a new VW, that is.

Impossible.

A Volkswagen can't boil over.

It's physically impossible.

The reason is absurdly simple: the VW's rear engine is cooled by air, not water.

Since air can't boil, neither can the car.

If you had to, you could drive a VW all day at top speed through a desert. Or edge along in bumper-to-bumper traffic on the hottest day of the year.

You may get all steamed up, but not your Volkswagen.

Chances are you'll appreciate the air-cooled engine even more in winter. Air can't freeze any more than it can boil. So you don't need anti-freeze. (You couldn't put any in a VW even if you wanted to; there's no radiator. And so no hoses to leak. No draining. No flushing. No rust.)

In the past, a few VW owners have been annoyed to find a perplexed gas station attendant with a bucket of water and no place to put it.

But we've taken care of that in our '61 model. This year, a windshield washer is standard equipment.

It uses water.

Let the man fill it up.

Our number one salesman.

Even people who have never been near a VW can tell you how good the service is.

It's more than just a reputation.

It's become a legend.

Once you've got a legend on your hands, you've got to live up to it. And we do.

VW dealers see to it that you get the same front-door treatment whether you're

buying a new car or just having your old one greased.

It's the kind of feeling you'd hope for if you drove up in a $5,000 car.

Only you don't have to hope for it.

Of course, the Volkswagen itself helps explain why our service is so good.

We don't make sweeping changes every

year and turn it into a mechanic's nightmare.

When a mechanic works on the same basic car year after year, it's no wonder he gets to know it inside out.

And so it's no wonder people keep coming back. With friends.

If that isn't a salesman, we don't know what is.

Lemon.

This Volkswagen missed the boat.

The chrome strip on the glove compartment is blemished and must be replaced. Chances are you wouldn't have noticed it; Inspector Kurt Kroner did.

There are 3,389 men at our Wolfsburg factory with only one job: to inspect Volkswagens at each stage of production. (3000 Volkswagens are produced daily; there are more inspectors than cars.)

Every shock absorber is tested (spot checking won't do), every windshield is scanned. VWs have been rejected for surface scratches barely visible to the eye.

Final inspection is really something! VW inspectors run each car off the line onto the Funktionsprüfstand (car test stand), tote up 189 check points, gun ahead to the automatic brake stand, and say "no" to one VW out of fifty.

This preoccupation with detail means the VW lasts longer and requires less maintenance, by and large, than other cars. (It also means a used VW depreciates less than any other car.)

We pluck the lemons; you get the plums.

"I don't want an imported car. I want a Volkswagen."

Someone actually said it.

A lady in Chicago.

She said it to one of our dealers in that city, Loop Import Motors.

Of course, the lady was mistaken; the Volkswagen *is* an imported car. But it was a revealing mistake. In those ten words, she summed up the special status of the Volkswagen in America today, and the reputation its dealers have for parts and service.

As a matter of fact, the Volkswagen dealer is as unique as the car itself.

He doesn't handle VWs as a sideline; he concentrates on this one make. But that's not all. He concentrates on one *model* that remains basically the same year after year. A tremendous advantage.

Let's take parts, for instance. Most parts for the Volkswagen are *interchangeable* from

Engine can be removed and replaced in 90 minutes.

one year to the next. Even when a part is improved (and improvements take place in the VW all the time), the new part is usually designed to fit previous-year Volkswagens as well!

Every Authorized Volkswagen Dealer is required to stock at least $12,000 worth of parts, which would be the equivalent of a $40,000 or $50,000 parts inventory for a make that comes out with a different model every year or two. (And these are conservative figures; most VW dealers stock two or three times the minimum in parts.)

This explains why it is actually easier to get parts for a Volkswagen than for many domestic cars on the road today.

Volkswagen parts are inexpensive. A new front fender is $21.75.* A cylinder with piston and rings, $16.55.* And you'll find labor

The same fender fits any year's Volkswagen.

charges equally reasonable, because the Volkswagen has been deliberately designed for easy, low-cost maintenance. The car is so well conceived that the engine can be removed and replaced in only 90 minutes.

Here's another reason why VW service is so good. The Volkswagen dealer lays out his whole operation to service the one basic model. All his equipment is designed to take care of the Volkswagen; even the hoist.

The mechanics are not only factory-trained, but they've been working on this one basic model year after year, so you'd expect them to know just about everything there is to know about the car. And they do.

If you see this shingle, he's an authorized dealer.

There's a difference in attitude too. You feel it the first time you bring your VW back to be serviced: you get the same front-door treatment that you got when you bought the car. As a matter of fact, the newer VW dealerships don't even have a back-door or side-door entrance for service; you go in through the *front* door to deal with the service advisor.

It's the kind of an attitude you'd expect to find if you were bringing in a $6,000 car to be serviced; you get it with a car that costs only $1,565.*

The VW could never have gotten where it is today without good service. We and our dealers intend to keep it that way.

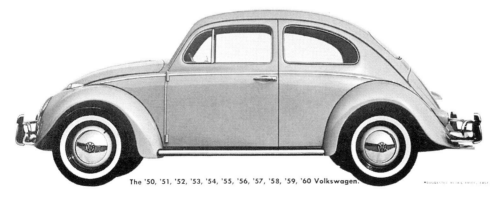

The '50, '51, '52, '53, '54, '55, '56, '57, '58, '59, '60 Volkswagen.

*SUGGESTED RETAIL PRICE, EAST COAST, P.O.E. ©1960 BY VOLKSWAGEN OF AMERICA, INC.

A Volkswagen, obviously.

It's easy to spot a Volkswagen.

Even with enough snow on it to hide the beetle shape.

It's the one that keeps moving.

A Volkswagen will even go up icy hills when other cars won't go at all because we put the engine in the back. It gives the rear wheels much better traction.

That's half the problem.

But the engine can't just be there. It has to keep working.

So we cool the VW engine with air, not water. There's no need for anti-freeze, no chance of the block cracking. (No possibility of boiling over in summer, either.) And there's no draining. No flushing. No rust.

You can park a VW outdoors in sub-zero weather or dig it out of a snowbank; it's ready to roll as soon as you turn the key.

If you happen to live where ice and snow are no problem, don't think you can't judge the VW's extraordinary abilities.

Just try it in sand or mud.

Volkswagen overdoes it again: 4 coats of paint.

Why four coats of paint when three would be more than enough?

For the same reason that we finish the inside of the Volkswagen door jamb like the outside of the car. And seal the underside of the VW so that it's more like a ship's bottom than a car bottom.

Who'll know the difference? We will.

Let's get back to that paint job.

First the VW is literally submerged in paint, bathed in it. Then baked, and sanded. Coat No. 2 is sprayed on. Baked. Then every visible inch is sanded by hand. Coat No. 3 sprayed on. Baked. Fully sanded again. Coat No. 4 sprayed on. Baked. Whew!

Incidentally, the fourth coat is an extra dividend the factory declared back in November. It gives the Volkswagen finish even more transparency and depth. (You don't look at it; you look into it.) And, of course, it's still another protective coat against the weather.

This is the sort of excess that makes a Volkswagen a Volkswagen.

No point showing the '62 Volkswagen. It still looks the same.

No heads will turn when you drive a '62 Volkswagen home.

Maybe an eagle-eyed neighbor will notice that we've made the tail lights a little bigger. But that's the only clue.

Everything is right where we left it in 61, including the price: $1,595.

Inside is another story.

We've put all our time and effort into improvements that matter.

The '62 VW runs more quietly. There are new clutch and brake cables, as well as new steering parts, that never need maintenance. Heater outlets front and rear for more even heating. Easier braking.

And 24 more.

One change is literally a gassér.

We've added a gas gauge. Our first.

A few technicians say this is an idle state. If the VW's sporting fuel, but the gas gauge may be more novel than you'd imagine. It will not only tell you whether your tank is 1/4 or full, it will prove you're driving a '62.

It could make '62 go down in VW history as the year of the big change.

Never.

We'd no sooner make an over-chromed, two-toned Volkswagen than we'd change the classic beetle shape.

It's not that the chromed version looks so bad, it just doesn't make the car work any better.

That's the rule of thumb we go by: we change the VW only to improve it, not to make last year's model look obsolete.

In 1961, for example, we were able to get more horsepower from our air-cooled engine without making it any bigger or less economical.

(One thing did get bigger this year, the tail lights.)

Everything on the VW happens for a reason; nothing is for show.

We can't even have a chrome piece that spells out our name.

We do have a little round emblem with our initials on it, though.

After all, we can't let 600,000 Americans go riding around in unidentified cars.

In 1949 we sold 2 Volkswagens in the U.S.A.

But the next year the Volkswagen really caught on. We sold 157.

See. You mustn't get discouraged.

It takes people a little time to get used to a new idea.

By 1960, the number of VWs in the United States had grown somewhat: 500,000.

In the last twelve months alone around 185,000 VWs were sold—including station wagons and trucks. 23% more than in '59.

But it isn't just the car they've been buying. They've been buying the VW dealer too (and his counterparts all over the U.S.).

People don't buy an imported car in those numbers unless they've looked into service.

And they're not bashful, either. They stick their heads out at red lights and ask VW owners about it, point blank. They come in for a look at the parts department.

And they must like what they see and hear.

Come to think of it, it's a good thing those two lone Americans who bought VWs back in 1949 were a little more adventurous!

You don't have to replace half the car.

A new front fender for your Volkswagen doesn't mean major surgery.

Just 10 bolts, and you're in business.

We made simple maintenance a part of the Volkswagen design while the car was still on the drawing board.

And we went a lot deeper than just replacing the fenders.

A VW dealer can remove and replace the whole engine in 90 minutes.

(If you wanted to keep the engine and replace the car, it would take a little longer. But it's possible. Every part is in stock or on tap.)

Of course, the VW dealer has an edge: most parts are interchangeable from one year to the next.

So if your 1951 VW needed a fender, it wouldn't be any more trouble (or expense) than if it were a 1961.

 If you did need to replace a whole Volkswagen, they cost just $1,595* each. Brand new.

And you get to pick a new color.

A Volkswagen dealer is a man of many parts.

5,008 parts, to be exact.
And most of them fit any VW ever made.
(Because most parts are interchangeable from one year to the next.)
Which gives the VW dealer an enormous edge.
He can repair any year Volkswagen you

happen to drive up in.
All the parts are on hand or in top.
This system also helps to explain why VW service is fast and cheap.
A fuel pump is $9.95.* A rear fender, $17.50.*
Plus installation.
(And that new fender doesn't mean major

surgery, either. Just 10 bolts.)
But what impresses people most about VW service is how the dealer treats them.
Like a customer. Even for a 10c fuse.
We build the Volkswagen like a $5,000 car, so why shouldn't it get serviced like one?

The inside is finished like the outside.

This is our idea of a grand opening.
We took a Volkswagen apart so that you can see for yourself what the inside looks like.
You won't find one dribble on the paint or one nick on the chrome. Not one wrinkle, not one missed stitch.
We've got a bevy of seamstresses to

make sure nothing zags when it should zig.
Maybe you think quality isn't something you can quite put your finger on. But just run that finger underneath the dashboard. Smooth?
Along the headliner. Smooth?
Under the door. Smooth?
Smooth.

It's one of our old family recipes: a lot of patience plus a lot of paint.
A visitor once asked, "4 coats of paint? Isn't that putting it on a bit thick?"
We said, "No."
We don't count on the paint to hold the VW together. But it keeps it from falling apart.

How can you be sure you're getting a '62?

Don't worry.
You couldn't buy a new '61 VW if you wanted to; there are none left.
Besides, there are some sure-fire ways to tell the '62 from any other year.
It just takes a little looking.
The taillights are half an inch bigger.
And the new VW also has a gas gauge.

But most of the changes can't be seen.
You feel them.
We've put new heater outlets both front and rear for more even heating.
Braking takes less pressure.
Brake, clutch and steering parts that once needed maintenance, don't any more.
Nothing on the VW can shift better.

So we've made a few things stay open better. Doorstops that work. A spring to hold the front hood open.
In all, there are 28 significant changes.
But not one of them makes last year's model obsolete.
And that's the way it'll be in '63, too.

And if you run out of gas, it's easy to push.

See?
We think of everything.
Getting a Volkswagen to the side of the road is a pushover.
It's a little surprising that VW owners don't run out of gas more often.
A figure like 32 miles to the gallon can make you a little hazy about when you

just filled up.
And you spend so little time in gas stations, there are almost no reminders.
You'll probably never need oil between changes, for example.
You'll never need water or anti-freeze because the engine is air-cooled.
40,000 miles and a set of tires won't break

any Volkswagen records.
And repairs are few and far between.
So this year we've installed a gas gauge to help you remember.
But we haven't taken all the fun away.
You still have to remember to look at it.

2 shapes known   the world over.

Nobody really notices Coke bottles or Volkswagens any more.

They're so well known, they blend in with the scenery. It doesn't matter what the scenery is, either. You can walk in and buy a VW in any one of 136 countries.

And that takes in lots of scenery.

Deserts. Mountains. Hot places. Cold places. Volkswagens thrive.

Hot and cold don't matter, the VW engine is air-cooled. It doesn't use water, so it can't freeze up or boil over.

And having the engine in the back makes all the difference when it comes to mud and sand and snow.

The weight is over the power wheels and so the traction is terrific.

VWs also get along so well wherever they are because our service is as good in Tasmania as it is in Toledo.

The only reason you can't buy a Volkswagen at the North Pole is that we won't sell you one. There's no VW service around the corner.)

We hear that it's possible to buy yourself a Coke at the North Pole, though.

Which makes us suspect there's only one thing that can get through ahead of a Volkswagen.

A Coke truck.

How to tell the year of a Volkswagen.

(It isn't easy. We never change it to make it look different, only to make it work better.)

1952-1955. '52 was the last year we split the rear window. In '53, the VW sprouted front window vents. And by '55, flashing directional signals replaced those funny-looking little arms.

1956 Or is it a '57? This one's tricky. Look for twin exhausts plus an oval rear window.

1957 No visible change.

1958 A famous Italian designer suggested we make the rear window bigger. We did.

1959 We changed the door handles from the pull type to the new push-button type.

1960 Look for the new medallion design on the front. (You may need your glasses.)

1961 Your clue is the windshield washer nozzle on the hood. (Standard equipment.)

1962 Bigger tail lights. Final proof. Peek inside. Only the '62s have a gas gauge.)

Our image.

Once upon a time, a young lady visited our plant. (In our view, the more the merrier.)

"What a sweet little car," she said. "It looks just like a beetle."

Now we're a pretty down-to-earth bunch.

At that moment we were figuring how much larger our brake-area would have to be if we stepped up our horsepower.

She stopped us cold.

After we'd made some discreet inquiries, we found out that a good many people shared her opinion.

But we also found out that people never said "beetle" nastily.

Always affectionately.

So we grew resigned to our nickname, and finally rather pleased with it.

It seems to say a lot about our attitude to car-making: determined, painstaking, unpretentious.

After all, some people try like mad to create a favorable impression.

We'd simply tried to make the Volkswagen a practical car.

And we'd gotten our very own image.

How to do a Volkswagen ad.

1. Look at the car.

2. Look harder. You'll find enough advantages to fill a lot of ads. Like the air-cooled engine, the economy, the design that never goes out of date.

3. Don't exaggerate. For instance, some people have gotten 50 m.p.g. and more from a VW. But others have only managed 28. Average: 32. Don't promise more.

4. Call a spade a spade. And a suspension a suspension. Not something like "orbital cushioning."

5. Speak to the reader. Don't shout. He can hear you. Especially if you talk sense.

6. Pencil sharp? You're on your own.

(Picture goes here.)

(Write headline here.)

(Start copy here.)

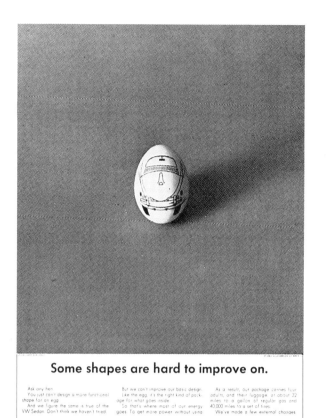

Some shapes are hard to improve on.

Ask any hen.
You just can't design a more functional shape for an egg.
And we figure the same is true of the VW Sedan. Don't think we haven't tried.

But we can't improve our basic design. Like the egg, it's the right kind of package for what goes inside.
So that's where most of our energy goes. To get more power without using

As a result, our package carries four adults, and their luggage, at about 32 miles to a gallon of regular gas and 40,000 miles to a set of tires.
We've made a few external changes

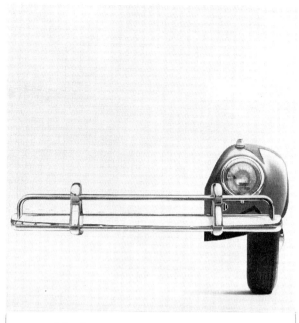

What if you only need part of a Volkswagen?

You're in luck.
Parts of Volkswagens are easier to get than whole ones.
Any part. For any year.
That's the nice thing about making the same car year-in and year-out.
You can spend your time fiddling with the insides instead of the outside.

We've made some 3,000 improvements in our little car and hundreds of them fit our oldest models, too.
(Did you know you can get parts for a 15-year-old VW faster than for some of the new jobs around?)
Volkswagen parts are also easy to install. For instance, our fenders are bolted

on. (10 bolts do it. So you don't have to replace half the car.)
And the whole engine can be replaced in an hour and a half.
Of course, as you think about this, you may prefer to get all our new parts at once.
We have such a package.

The 1962½ Volkswagen.

When we find a way to improve the Volkswagen, we do it.
Then and there.
If you went out to buy a new VW today, you'd get one with an entirely new steering mechanism.
It gives you an even better sense of

touch with the road and makes the VW still easier to handle.
We weren't in any rush to put it in our '62 model, it wasn't quite ready.
And we're not waiting for the '63 VW to come out; it's ready now.
We've made thousands of changes in

the past 15 years. But not one has ever made a VW obsolete; only better.
People sometimes ask us why we don't change our car once a year like everybody else.
The answer is simple: once a year isn't always enough.

Our philosophy.

We have a very simple philosophy.
It's merely a matter of questioning what people have always taken for granted.
Here's how it works:
Just because everybody else put the horsepower in front doesn't mean we had to.
(Anyone who's driven a Volkswagen in snow or mud knows where the horsepower works best. Over the drivewheels.)
Just because we sell cars doesn't put selling at the top of our agenda.
(For us, service comes first.)

Just because this is big-car country, we haven't assumed that nobody wants a small car.
(That's how the "small-car revolution" started.)
Just because most people change models, shapes, sizes, trims and so forth every year, we don't have to follow suit.
(We figure the way a car works is far more important than the way it looks.)
Back in '49 when there were just two VWs in the whole U.S.A., this way of thinking must have seemed pretty cranky.
But now?

Think small.

Our little car isn't so much of a novelty any more.

A couple of dozen college kids don't try to squeeze inside it.

The guy at the gas station doesn't ask where the gas goes.

Nobody even stares at our shape.

In fact, some people who drive our little flivver don't even think 32 miles to the gallon is going any great guns.

Or using five pints of oil instead of five quarts.

Or never needing anti-freeze.

Or racking up 40,000 miles on a set of tires.

That's because once you get used to some of our economies, you don't even think about them any more.

Except when you squeeze into a small parking spot. Or renew your small insurance. Or pay a small repair bill. Or trade in your old VW for a new one.

Think it over.

It makes your house look bigger.

Cars are getting to be bigger, so houses are getting to look smaller.

But one little Volkswagen can put everything back in its proper perspective.

A VW parked in front does big things for your house. And your garage. To say nothing of small parking spots and narrow roads.

On the other hand, a VW does make some things smaller.

Gas bills, for instance. (At 32 mpg, they'll probably be half what you pay now.)

You'll probably never add oil between changes. You'll certainly never need antifreeze. Tires go 40,000 miles. And even insurance costs less.

One thing you'd think might be smaller

in a Volkswagen is the inside.

But there's as much legroom in front of a VW as there is in the biggest cars.

When you think about it, you really have only two choices:

You can buy a bigger house for who-knows-how-much.

Or a Volkswagen for $1,595.*

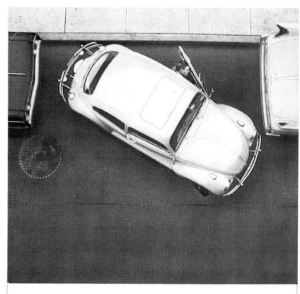

If you wouldn't own a car in New York City, maybe you should buy a Volkswagen.

We aren't going to tell you it's fun to own a VW in New York City.

It's hard to own any kind of car here.

But a VW can take out some of the bumps.

Take parking. You can take leftovers. (Or if you rent garage space by the month, you can often get it for less money because a VW takes up less room.)

A VW can't get you out of a jam on the FDR Drive. But at least you won't idle away as much gas as the guy behind you. (And no matter how mad you get, you'll never boil over. Be-

cause a VW has no radiator.)

And if the bumper-to-bumper crosstown traffic gets one of your fenders, you don't have to replace half your car.

In fact, a whole brand-new VW costs only $1639,* gets about 27 mpg, holds 5 pints of oil instead of 5 quarts, goes 40,000 miles on tires, and costs less for insurance and license plates.

So you not only get all the good things about owning a VW in New York.

You get all the good things about owning a VW, period.

Made in U.S.A.

George H. Long, of Grand Rapids, Mich., made this Volkswagen out of spare parts in his spare time.

The car runs very well.

But not often.

Mr. Long uses it to teach VW mechanics at one of our training schools.

They tear it to pieces and put it together

again. And again. And again.

After suffering this kind of education, our mechanics get to be pretty sharp.

(So does our service.)

Of course, we admit that our car is easier to learn about than most.

Because we don't make drastic changes every year. And because the changes we

do make, make sense.

This policy has another advantage:

Since most VW parts are interchangeable from year to year, you can easily get parts for any Volkswagen.

You'll find this comforting.

If you're building your own VW.

Or buying one ready made.

$1.02 a pound.

A new Volkswagen costs $1,595.

But that isn't as cheap as it sounds. Pound for pound a VW costs more than practically any car you can name.

Actually, that isn't too surprising when you look into it.

Not many cars get as much put into them as a Volkswagen.

The hand work alone is striking.

VW engines are put together by hand. One by one.

And every engine is tested twice: once when it's still an engine and again when it's part of the finished car.

A Volkswagen gets painted 4 times and sanded by hand between each coat.

Even the roof lining is hand-fitted.

You won't find a nick or a dimple or a

blob of glue on a VW because we aren't above rejecting a piece of car for a whole car if we have to.

So you can see why a Volkswagen is so expensive when you figure it by the pound.

It's something to think about.

Particularly if you haven't bought one because you thought they didn't cost enough.

33 years later, he got the bug.

We're glad that most people don't wait 33 years to buy their first Volkswagen.

But Albert Gillis did, and maybe he had the right idea all along.

He didn't buy a new car for 33 years because he didn't happen to need one.

He and his 1929 Model A Ford did just fine by each other.

He always did his own repairs and even jacked it up at night to save the tires.

When he needed a new car last year, he went out and bought a Volkswagen.

"I heard they hold up," he explained. Does he like the VW?

Mr. Gillis is 78, a Justice of the Peace, and not given to hasty decisions.

"Your inspectors sure do a good job of inspecting," was as far as he would go.

But he did mention that he and Mrs. Gillis took a trip for their 54th anniversary.

They drove 6,750 miles and spent $62 on gas and 55¢ on oil.

"I didn't think they were supposed to burn oil," he said.

The green fender came
    off a '58.
The blue hood came
    off a '59.
The beige fender came
    off a '64.
The turquoise door came
    off a '62.
Most VW parts
    are interchangeable
    from one year to the next.
That's why parts
    are so easy to get.

1

Open on snow covered
landscape in early morning
darkness.

MVO:

Have you ever wondered

2

how the man who drives the
snowplough drives to the
snowplough?

3

This one drives a Volkswagen.

4

So you can stop wondering.

Snowplough

1

Open on VW pulling up at the
foot of a very grand building.

MVO:

The Volkswagen is one of the
tallest cars in the world.

2

So there's more than enough
head room.

3

4

Even for the little woman.

Little Woman

That's how many times we inspect a Volkswagen.

These are some of the ok's our little car has to get in our factory.

(It's easy to tell the ok's from the no's. One no is all you ever see.)

We pay 5,857 men just to look for things to say no to.

And no is no.

A visitor from Brazil once asked us what we were going to do about a roof that came through with a dent in it.

Dents are easy to hammer out.

So what we did shook him a little.

We smashed the body down to a metal lump and threw it out in the scrap pile.

We stop VWs for little things that you may never notice yourself.

The fit of the lining in the roof.

The finish in a doorjamb.

In the final inspection alone, our VW has to get through 342 points without one blackball.

One out of 50 doesn't make it.

But you should see the ones that get away.

There are no real Volkswagen taxis. But there is one very good fake.

Think it over, New York, Chicago, San Francisco.

We drove our Volkswagen taxi through town on the way to get its picture taken.

And did we stop traffic!

You'd think it was the first sensible thing people had ever seen. And maybe it was.

A VW is 4 feet shorter than other cabs.

So a whole fleet of them is as good as getting miles of extra streets for free.

Because they're shorter, VWs get out of the way quicker. So traffic doesn't get all balled up while some lady hunts for a 5c tip.

The people who'd run Volkswagens could buy a lot more cabs for their money and run each one for a lot less, too.

They wouldn't need antifreeze in winter and they could forget about boiling over in

summer; the VW engine is air-cooled.

Above all, the two passengers and the driver of a VW cab would have more fun than any other three people in town.

It may sound peculiar to you to stand on a corner and yell, "Volkswagen!"

But it sounds beautiful to us.

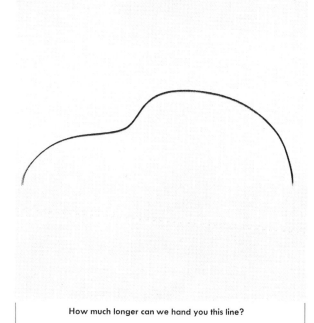

How much longer can we hand you this line?

Forever, we hope.

Because we don't ever intend to change the Volkswagen's shape.

We play by our own set of rules.

The only reason we change the VW is to make it work even better.

The money we don't spend on outside changes we do spend inside the car.

This system gives us an immense advantage: Time.

We have time to improve parts and still keep most of them interchangeable.

(Which is why it's so easy to get VW parts, and why VW mechanics don't wake up screaming.)

We have time to put an immense amount

of hand work into each VW, and to finish each one like a $6,000 machine.

And this system has also kept the price almost the same over the years.

Some cars keep changing and stay the same.

Volkswagens stay the same and keep changing.

Three ideas that shook the automotive world.

Mass production (Ford's Model T): "Any color you want, as long as it's black," was the theory. Henry Ford built one standard model that almost everyone could afford to buy. The "T" put the country on wheels.

Streamlining (Chrysler's Airflow): The Airflow was the first new car that looked like a new car. It was a magnificent flop in 1934 because it was way ahead of its time. But it left its mark on every car since.

The small car (Volkswagen's Volkswagen): The VW came along and offered a sensible size, low price, high gas mileage, utter reliability, careful workmanship and a shape that was always in style. You can still get one.

This is why

a Volkswagen has so much legroom in front.

A Volkswagen has so much legroom in front because the engine is in back, out of the way.

How much is so much?

Believe it or not, a little VW has as much legroom as most of the biggest cars around.

As much legroom, in fact, as a limousine.

A limousine, mind you!

(And just as an aside, there's even more headroom in a VW than in a limousine.)

Frankly, we didn't put the VW engine in back just to get more legroom in front.

The original idea was to put the weight of the engine over the back wheels to get much better traction.

A Volkswagen goes where other cars won't go, even without snow tires.

So you forge ahead, with your engine behind you and your legs stretched out in front.

If you have very long legs and like to drive in the snow wearing a top hat, you might give the VW some thought.

Any change will be an improvement.

All we do when we change the Volkswagen is to make it work even better.

We don't play with the way it looks. So the 1965 VW still looks the same.

And there you have the whole Volkswagen point of view:

We keep looking for ways to improve it. And then we knock our brains out to make the new pieces fit old VWs, too.

All the improvements make a fat book. And every one has made the car a touch better than it was before.

This year, for example, all the windows are bigger. There's more legroom in back. The heater/defroster has been improved. And so have the brakes.

Even the jack has been redesigned.

This system not only makes the VW better all the time, but also makes parts easier to get, mechanics more skillful and owners always in style.

And we can still sell it for $1,595.*

Keep the change.

Why is our top so way out?

The top of the Volkswagen Convertible is way out of the car for a very simple reason: We had no other practical place to put it.

Of course, we had other alternatives.

We could have put the top in the back seat. (It wouldn't have been out of the car, but 2 or 3 people would have been.)

Or we could have made room for the top by making the bug a little longer. (But it would no longer have been the little bug.)

The way it worked out, our Convertible has all the practical benefits of our Sedan: Seating for 4 adults, parking ease, and economy (average 32 mpg; 40,000 miles on tires).

But many people don't need practical benefits. They simply like our top.

They like it because it has a real glass window in back. And because it's padded, stitched, and fitted by hand, so it's weatherproof and it actually cushions sound.

They like our top when it's up for its smooth custom-made look. And they like it when it's down for its unusual way-out look.

To many people our top is so way-out, it's in.

Open on set of TV game show.

Announcer:

As you'll remember, last week Gino Milano, our little shoemaker here, successfully answered all the questions on his chosen category, cars.

This week he's back to tell us whether or not he'll step up to the big plateau.

Gino, the higher you go the harder they get.

What is your decision?

Gino: I go.

Announcer:

Okay, he goes.
Gino Milano, shoemaker, car expert, look to your left. Here is the brand new 1968 Volkswagen. How many changes can you find? You have ten seconds.

Time's up, Gino.
How many changes are there?

Gino: None.
SFX: Claxon.
MVO:

Poor Gino, he was done in by the 1968 Volkswagen and the 36 nice little changes that made this short programme possible.

Gino

They said it couldn't be done.
It couldn't.

We tried. Lord knows we tried. But no amount of pivoting or faking could squeeze the Philadelphia 76ers' Wilt Chamberlain into the front seat of a Volkswagen.

So if you're 7'1" tall like Wilt, our car is not for you.

But maybe you're a mere 6'7".

In that case, you'd be small enough to appreciate what a big thing we've made of the Volkswagen.

There's more headroom than you'd expect. (Over 37½" from seat to roof.)

And there's more legroom in front than you'd get in a limousine. Because the engine's tucked over the rear wheels where it's out of the way (and where it can give the most traction).

You can put 2 medium-sized suitcases up front (where the engine isn't), and 3 fair-sized kids in the back seat. And you can sleep an enormous infant in back of the back seat.

Actually, there's only one part of a VW that you can't put much into.

The gas tank.

But you can get about 29 miles per gallon out of it.

Presenting America's slowest fastback.

There are some new cars around with very streamlined roofs.

But they are not Volkswagens.

They are called fastbacks, and some of them are named after fish.

You can tell them from Volkswagens because a VW won't go over 72 mph. (Even though the speedometer shows a wildly optimistic top speed of 90.)

So you can easily break almost any speed law in the country in a VW.

And you can also cruise right past gas stations, repair shops and tire stores.

The VW engine may not be the fastest, but it's among the most advanced. It's made of magnesium alloy (one step better than aluminum). And it's so well machined you may never add oil between changes.

The VW engine is cooled by air, so it can never freeze up or boil over.

It won't have anything to do with water.

So we saw no reason to name it after a fish.

Take it for a test drive. See if you pass.

The real test in a Volkswagen is to see if you know what driving really is.

(If you think you're driving in other cars, then what you do in a Volkswagen is something else.)

Most cars give you all the lively moving sensation of sitting on your living room couch.

But the VW isn't sprung like other cars. Its 4-wheel torsion bar suspension (the kind they have in racers) gives you the feel of the road.

You always know what's going on because you know what your car's going on.

And you know what's coming, because you'll see more road than you ever saw before. (Our sloping hood doesn't cut off your view.)

When you twist the steering wheel a little, you can feel the front wheels turn a little. So you know the car's doing just what you told it to. (Doesn't that sound satisfying?)

We can tell you that the Volkswagen parks shorter than other cars, and that it maneuvers more easily.

But we can't tell you how it feels to drive one.

So take the test.

Maybe you can tell us.

Some of the fastest cars in the world   are still following the Volkswagen.

A Volkswagen is O.K. for racing down to the delicatessen, but that's about it.

Still, it may be some consolation to know that Volkswagens have a lot in common with cars that race for a living.

Item: Each VW wheel has its own private suspension system, complete with its own private torsion bar.

So when one wheel goes klunk on a bump, the other wheels do nothing at all. They stick to the road, and so does the car.

Many racing cars use this suspension system. No other passenger car does.

Item: The Volkswagen engine is in the back, over the drive wheels. It gives the car better traction and doesn't waste power. Not all racing cars have engines in the back. Only every winner at Indianapolis this year.

Item: Just about every racing car has an aluminum engine. Aluminum is very light. Volkswagens have aluminum-magnesium engines that make aluminum alone seem heavy.

Item: The Volkswagen's 4-speed transmission is so smooth, some racing drivers use it "as is" in their cars. (Attention VW Accounting Department: Now you know why we sold more transmissions than cars last year.)

Of course, most of what we put into the VW isn't just for the sake of speed.

We keep trying to make it easier to drive, cheaper to run, simpler to service and longer lasting.

A Volkswagen may have a top speed of only 72 miles an hour.

But it's way ahead of cars that are way ahead of it.

Doyle Dane Bernbach Inc.

1

Open on shot of Middle Eastern
country.

MVO:
There's a little country in
the Middle East with just about
the most oil of any place in
the world.
And therefore just about the
most money per person and the
most cars per person of any
place in the world.

2

But regrettably, very few
Volkswagens.

With all that oil who needs a
Volkswagen because it doesn't
take much oil or gas.

3

With all that money, who needs
a Volkswagen because it doesn't
cost much. And with all that
parking space, who needs a
Volkswagen because it's so
easy to park. So a country
like this doesn't need
Volkswagens.

4

But what about an
undeveloped country. Like
America.

Lawrence of Arabia

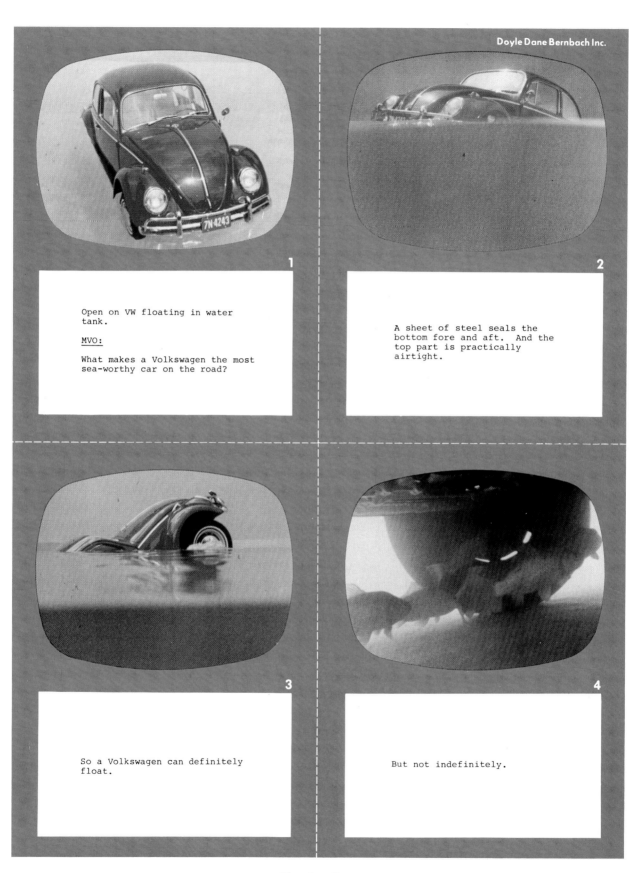

Doyle Dane Bernbach Inc.

1

Open on VW floating in water
tank.

<u>MVO:</u>

What makes a Volkswagen the most
sea-worthy car on the road?

2

A sheet of steel seals the
bottom fore and aft. And the
top part is practically
airtight.

3

So a Volkswagen can definitely
float.

4

But not indefinitely.

Floating Car

How to make a '54 look like a '64.

Paint it.

See? It looks like next year's model.

And next year's model looks like last year's model. And so it goes.

VWs always look the same because we change the car only to make it work better, never to make it look different.

So the people who bought '63 VWs aren't nervous about what the '64s will look like. And neither are we.

We've made over 5 million Volkswagens and we're still making changes.

Not enough to make you run out and buy a new one every year.

But enough to notice the differences when you do. (14 changes for '64 alone.)

In the meantime, no matter what year VW you own, you can always get parts easily; many of them are interchangeable from one year to the next.

So if you like, you can keep your old VW running forever.

Just spray it every few years.

Old paint rides again.

Ugh.

This is an awful picture of a Volkswagen. It's just not us.

We don't go in much for trading bees or sales jamborees or assorted powwows.

Maybe it's because we don't quite understand the system.

We've never figured out why they run clearance sales on brand new cars.

If there are cars left over every year, why make so many in the first place?

And how come the price goes down, even though the cars are still brand new?

How does the poor guy who bought one last week feel about this week's prices?

How can a dealer keep enough parts on hand when they all keep changing?

How can a mechanic keep track of what he's doing?

It's all very confusing.

Either we're, way behind the times. Or way ahead.

Mr. Kennedy and his 1947, 1955, 1956, 1958, 1961, 1962, 1963, 1965 Volkswagen.

As long as Michael Kennedy can remember, there's always been a bug around the house.

In all, his family has owned about 15 VWs. (give or take a few aunts and uncles).

So when Mr. Kennedy decided to buy one for himself, he knew enough about it to have a little fun.

He bought the body of a '47 VW and the chassis of a '55 VW. And put them together.

Then he added a '55 engine, '55 doors, '56 seats, '58 bumpers, '61 tail lights, a '62 fender, a '63 front end and a '65 transmission. (Plus a few more odds and ends.)

The 18 years' difference between the oldest part and the newest part didn't make any difference.

Many VW parts are interchangeable from one year to the next. (So there'll never be any part we can't replace in a hurry.)

If you'd rather not buy a VW the do-it-yourself way, don't worry.

At no extra charge, we'll do it ourselves.

It comes in three economy sizes.

These are just some of the sizes Volkswagens come in. Regular, large and giant economy size.

The one on the right, our big bus-like box, and the one in the center, our medium sized Squareback sedan, are only about 7 inches longer than the beetle.

But don't let their size on the outside fool you about their size in the inside.

Just open a door and you'll find enough room for more than enough things.

Then there's the familiar bug.

While it's not as big as the other two Volkswagens, it has plenty of room for 4 people and a small dog. Plus a suitcase for everybody but the dog.

All three Volkswagens do everything you expect from a Volkswagen. Except look silly. One of them (the Squareback) looks exactly like a car. They have air-cooled engines in the rear that won't freeze up in the winter or boil over in the summer.

They won't use any anti-freeze and are very easy on gasoline. (The bug and the Squareback average about 27 miles on a gallon of gas. The box about 23 miles.)

And they all go about 35 to 40,000 miles on a set of tires.

So you see, no matter what size we make VWs they're all pretty economical.

Why not come in and size one up?

Slightly convertible.

Some people can't ride in a regular convertible without trying to convert it. "Put the top down, Daddy." "Leave it up, Harry."

You can't make a compromise. (Try driving a regular convertible with the top only halfway up.) But you can buy one.

The Volkswagen Sunroof Sedan.

The Sunroof is a cross between a VW Sedan and a VW Convertible. It has a hole in the roof, with a steel cover that cranks open to give you 390 square inches of sky.

Or 389 square inches of sky. Or ½ square inch. Or whatever's comfortable.

And if no opening is comfortable, you can have that roof just crank the cover closed until it pops up against its sealing gasket.

This makes our Sunroof as air-tight and water-tight as our Sedan.

The cover is padded and lined like the rest of the roof, so you can hardly see it.

Some people can hardly see paying an extra $90* for it, either. (Until they take a VW Sunroof out on the road. And open her up.)

Even the bottom of a Volkswagen looks funny.

Has the Volkswagen fad died out?

You're missing a lot when you own a Volkswagen.

The first car at the bottom of the world.

Doyle Dane Bernbach Inc.

1

Open on spinning wheel of car stuck in snow.

VW owner:

Hi. Need a lift?

Other driver:

Oh, thanks. I don't know what's wrong.
That's a wonderful car I have back there. Did you notice?

2

VW owner:

Yeh.

Other driver:

It's loaded. Everything they sell. Power brakes, power steering, power windows, power seats, power radio antenna.

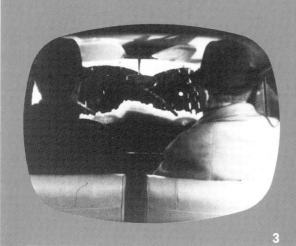

3

VW owner:
Mmm.

Other driver:

And it rides like a dream. Oh, it'll do 120 easy. 400 horses, you know. You have no idea what a sense of power that gives you. And it all works on push buttons.

Say, you're a nice guy.

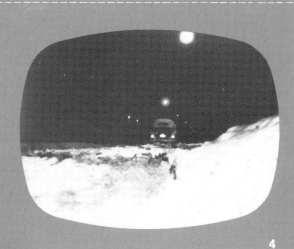

4

VW owner:

Well, I...

Other driver:

Too bad you have to drive this little thing. I'm going to let you take mine for a spin. As soon as winter's over.

Spinning Wheel

Does the stickshift scare your wife?

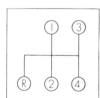

The way the stick shifts

We wouldn't be a bit surprised to learn that the stickshift is all that stands between your wife and a Volkswagen.

She hasn't touched a gearshift in years (maybe not in her life), so why start struggling with one now?

In the first place, it's not a struggle any more. Because the VW has synchromesh on all 4 gears to let you slide easily from one speed to another. In fact, our synchromesh is so smooth that, even if you've never done any stick shifting, you won't ever have to worry about our shift sticking.

You get better control on slippery roads. Because when you shift down, the motor helps to slow the car. You don't have to hit the brakes as often, so there's less chance of skidding.

The stickshift saves your money, too. (The VW could never average 32 miles per gallon if it had to waste engine power on slippage in an automatic transmission.)

Our fourth gear is really overdrive. When you're whizzing along the highway in fourth, the engine doesn't have to work as hard. Which saves wear and tear (and even more gas).

But a lot of people don't care about the practical aspects. They just want a stickshift for the fun of it. (That's not as weird as it might seem. What's the good of being in the driver's seat if the car does all the driving?)

Some drivers even pay extra to have a 4-speed synchromesh stickshift installed in their domestic cars. But, they still won't get a transmission as smooth as ours unless they do what many auto racers do: First, go out and buy a Volkswagen transmission from one of our dealers. And then, build the car around it.

If you still can't sell your wife on a VW, there's one more thing you can tell her about our stickshift:

After you use it for a couple of days, it becomes automatic.

The package it comes in

Ugly is only skin-deep.

It may not be much to look at. But beneath that humble exterior beats an air-cooled engine. It won't boil over and ruin your piston rings. It won't freeze over and ruin your life. It's in the back of the car for better traction in snow and sand. And it will give you about 29 miles to a gallon of gas.

After a while you get to like so much about the VW, you even get to like what it looks like.

You find that there's enough legroom for almost anybody's legs. Enough headroom for almost anybody's head. With a hat on it. Snug-fitting bucket seats. Doors that close so well you can hardly close them. (They're so airtight, it's better to open the window a crack first.)

Those plain, unglamorous wheels are each suspended independently. So when a bump makes one wheel bounce, the bounce doesn't make the other wheel bounce. It's things like that you pay the $1585* for, when you buy a VW. The ugliness doesn't add a thing to the cost of the car. That's the beauty of it.

©Volkswagen of America, Inc. *Suggested Retail Price, East Coast P.O.E. Local Taxes and Other Dealer Delivery Charges, if Any, Additional.

Don't let the low price scare you off.

$1,574.*

That's the price of a new Volkswagen.

But some people won't buy one. They feel they deserve something costlier. That's the price we pay for the price we charge.

And some people are afraid to buy one: They don't see how we can turn out a cheap car without having it turn out cheap. This is how.

Since the factory doesn't change the bug's shape every year, we don't have to change the factory every year.

What we don't spend on looks, we spend on improvements to make more people buy the car.

Mass production cuts costs. And VWs have been produced in a greater mass (over 10 million to date) than any car model in history.

Our air-cooled rear engine cuts costs, too, by eliminating the need for a radiator, water pump, and drive shaft.

There are no fancy gadgets, run by push buttons.

(The only push buttons are on the doors. And those gadgets are run by you.)

When you buy a VW, you get what you pay for. What you don't get is frills. And you don't pay for what you don't get.

What if it poops out in Paducah?

A thing like that could happen, even to a Volkswagen. After all, it's only human.

And with your luck, it would happen at least 500 miles from home. In Paducah (Ky.) or Brewer (Me.) or Ketchikan (Alas.). Alas.

You may be far from happy, but you'll never be far from a VW dealer. We have one in each of those towns (and in

804 others in 50 states).

So if you want to find out how good VW service is, break down and call us.

You won't wait long for parts. All 5,008 are on hand or on tap.

And when we improve a part, we try to make it fit our older cars too. So a '64 clutch, for instance, is right at home in a '53 VW.

And the mechanic won't need all day to install the clutch the way he would for most cars). Our car is made so the work only takes 2 hours. And many repairs are finished even faster.

Because we designed the Volkswagen as if we expected it to poop out every week. And then we built it so it wouldn't.

Do you earn too much to afford one?

For many people the Volkswagen would be an ideal car. Except for one thing. It doesn't cost enough.

They're afraid nobody will know they have any money, if it doesn't show in their car. In other words, they buy their car for other people. Not themselves.

Then there are those who earn enough to buy a much better car than the VW. But they don't. Because they can't find one.

For them the best car is one that simply gets them there. Comfortably and economically. One they don't have to worry about. That doesn't make many stops for gas and rarely needs repairs.

A car where rare repairs don't cost very much. A car where the car doesn't even cost very much.

They feel they can afford to save money with a Volkswagen.

Now next time you see somebody driving a VW don't feel sorry for him.

Who knows? Someday the bank might be using his money to give you a new car loan.

Don't laugh.

A Volkswagen police car may seem like a funny idea to you, but it makes a lot of sense to the city of Scottsboro, Alabama.

They wanted a car that could take Police Officer H. L. Wilkerson on parking meter patrol; all day, 6 days a week, in stop-and-go traffic. Without breaking down. And without breaking the taxpayers.

So, in 1964, they bought Car S-5: a VW with a dome light, siren, and 2-way radio.

That was the year of Scottsboro's only 12" snowfall. The other police cars were in trouble up to their hubcaps. But Car S-5 was a credit to the Force. It went uphill. And downhill. And Officer Wilkerson didn't even bother to put the chains on.

Officer Wilkerson isn't supposed to go after speeders. But one day (in 1965) he chased one. And caught him. It's hard to say who was more surprised.

Car S-5 still averages 29 miles per gallon. It still doesn't use any oil between changes. And it's never had a breakdown.

After a year and a half of continuous use, it had its clutch replaced, and its valves adjusted. That is all.

Introducing two of the most radical changes in Volkswagen history. Can you spot them?

Did you notice that the headlights are vertical now instead of leaning back a bit? That doesn't make the car look any better. But it makes the road look better by making the lights a little brighter.

And that little hump in the back? We did that to hold the license plate up straight so the police can read it better. (Sorry.)

What you won't notice without driving the new model are the big improvements.

The engine has been enlarged to a fe-

rocious 53 horsepower. That only adds 3 m.p.h. to the top speed. Because we put most of the additional power where it would make the engine accelerate faster, turn slower and last even longer.

Now that the VW is getting to be such a hot car, we put in a couple of things to slow it down: Dual brakes.

The front wheel brakes are completely independent of the rear wheel brakes. So if you ever lost the front wheel brakes,

you could still stop the back of the car. (Which automatically stops the front too.)

The new VW also has seat belts, back-up lights and recessed door handles as standard equipment. In fact, this year we made so many changes on the VW that we thought we'd better make one more.

We wrote "Volkswagen" on the back of the car to be sure everybody would know what it was.

Volkswagen's unique construction keeps dampness out.

For years there have been rumors about floating Volkswagens. (The photographer claims this one stayed up for 42 minutes.) Why not?

The bottom of the Volkswagen isn't like ordinary car bottoms. A sheet of flat steel runs underneath the car, sealing the bottom fore and aft.

That's not done to make a bad boast out of it, just a better car. The sealed bottom protects a VW from water, dirt and salt. All the nasty things on the road that eventually eat up a car.

The top part of a Volkswagen is also very seaworthy. It's practically airtight. So airtight that it's hard to close the door

without rolling down the window a bit.

But there's still one thing to keep in mind if you own a Volkswagen. Even if it could definitely float, it couldn't float indefinitely.

So drive around the big puddles. Especially if they're big enough to have a name.

The most economical thing about a VW is how long it's economical.

This VW went 67,000 miles. And back.

Unless you've been marooned on a desert island, you probably know the Volkswagen has quite a reputation for being cheap to run.

As a matter of fact, a lot of VW owners have turned into crashing bores by talking endlessly about it.

It may be boring, but it's true.

Almost everyone gets about 29 miles to a gallon of regular gas. (Some get a bit more or a bit less depending on where and how they drive.)

It doesn't take much oil to keep a Volkswagen going. And tires that go 40,000 miles per set is no special news. (They're built to carry almost twice the weight of the car.)

The secret of more tire wear: more tire.

There aren't a lot of repairs and adjustments to put up with, either.

Parts don't cost a fortune because so many of them are interchangeable from one year to the next.

And license plates and insurance generally cost less than for other cars.

All in all, a Volkswagen can save you a good $200 a year.

Not bad.

But the thing that really sets the VW apart from other cars is its low depreciation.

The difference is staggering.

The fact is, domestic cars depreciate 2 times as fast as a Volkswagen in only one year.

A one-year-old VW that cost about $1,700* now is actually worth more than many year-old domestic cars that originally cost $2,100.

Stick around; it gets worse.

A 5-year-old Volkswagen could be sold for as much as $900 if it's in reasonably good shape.

But that 5-year-old $2,100 car is now worth maybe $400-$500. Maybe.

So it doesn't take an Einstein to figure out what an ugly hole depreciation can put in your pocket.

Unless you buy a Volkswagen.

And one Volkswagen may be the only one you'll ever have to buy.

Say you buy a 1966 VW for $1,700.*

And say you save that $200 on running it every year and put it in the bank.

In 5 years or so, you can take that car (if it's in reasonable shape) together with the money you've saved to your local friendly

Volkswagen dealer.

Chances are you can drive out with a brand-new VW and not have to add a dime.

One of the nice things about owning it is selling it.

If you don't like that idea, there's another alternative.

Buy a '66 VW and just drive it.

No one will stop you from keeping the same VW for as long as you like. (No one will know the difference anyway; we never change the way it looks.)

So you can just go on saving all that nice money year after year and get rich.

Maybe the VW really can't make a poor man rich. But neither can it make a rich man poor.

*Depending on accessories, local taxes and delivery charges.

One of the nice things about owning it is selling it.

A new Volkswagen doesn't depreciate wildly the minute you turn the key.

In a sense, the older it gets the more valuable it gets.

So that in 5 years, the same VW will be worth more than some 5-year-old cars that cost twice as much to begin with.

Old VWs are worth a lot because a lot of people want them.

One reason is that it takes a real car nut to tell a clean used one from a new one.

VWs always look like VWs.

Another reason is that they hold up.

A VW is put together so well, it's practically airtight. (It helps to open a window to close a door. Even on old ones.)

Then there's this: All the nice money you save with a new VW (on gas, oil, repairs, tires) you keep saving with an old one.

So you can get a nice price for it. (If something forces you to sell.)

It's the kind of economy that people are willing to pay an arm and a leg for.

Will we ever kill the bug?

Never.

How could we?

We brought the Volkswagen into the world, and gave it the best years of our life.

When people laughed at its looks, we helped it make friends all over the world. 8 million of them.

And we promised them that this was one car that would never go out of style (much less out of sight).

We won't deny that the bug's been changed. But not so you'd notice.

The 5,000-odd changes we've made since 1948 don't do a thing to the VW ex-cept make it work better and longer.

A few purists feel we kill the bug each time we improve it. But we have no choice.

We've got to keep killing the bug every chance we get.

That's the only sure way to keep it from dying.

1

Open on car transporter driving
through the night.

MVO:

It's here. New car time 1969.
And this year the new car boys
have put together something
really special.

2

Thirty Six hundred pounds of
precision built machinery.
Longer than a limousine, seats
eight, four big doors, twelve
big windows.

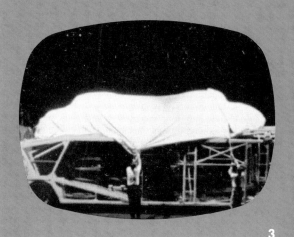

3

Not one heater. Two.
Not one rear window defroster.
Two. Not one radiator. None.
But what makes this package
really special, it costs no
more than the average automobile.

4

And goes in two different
directions at once.

New Car Time

After we paint the car we paint the paint.

You should see what we do to a Volkswagen even before we paint it.

We bathe it in steam, we bathe it in alkali, we bathe it in phosphate. Then we bathe it in a neutralizing solution.

If it got any cleaner, there wouldn't be much left to paint.

Then we dunk the whole thing into a vat of slate gray primer until every square inch of metal is covered. Inside and out.

Only one domestic car maker does this. And his cars sell for 3 or 4 times as much as a Volkswagen.

(We think that the best way to make an economy car is expensively.)

After the dunking, we bake it and sand it by hand.

Then we paint it.

Then we bake it again, and sand it again by hand.

Then we paint it again.

And bake it again.

And sand it again by hand.

So after 3 times, you'd think we wouldn't bother to paint it again and bake it again. Right?

Wrong.

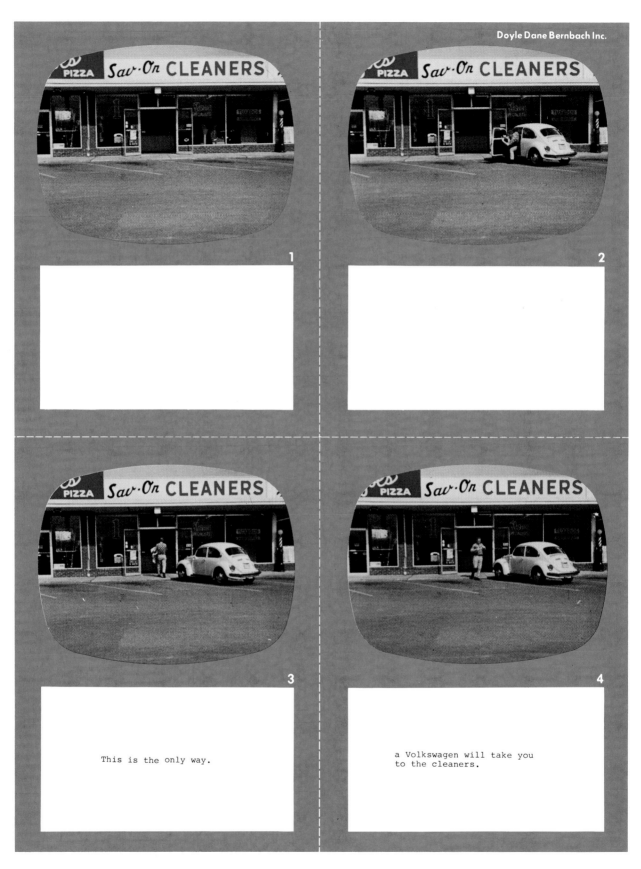

This is the only way.

a Volkswagen will take you
to the cleaners.

To The Cleaners

Doyle Dane Bernbach Inc.

MVO:

This is a dramatisation of a true story.

On November 28th 1970 a terrible storm developed in the Sierra Nevada mountains.

Dissolve to workmen clearing road.

MVO:

Six months later, when emergency crews cleared the road something strange happened. A car was found.

A Volkswagen. Buried beneath tons of snow and ice. But even stranger than that - when the crew supervisor turned the ignition key.....

SFX: Car engine starting first time. Then driving off.

The Storm

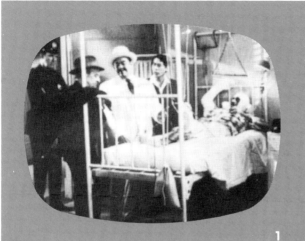

1

Open on hospital room.

No. 1 son:

Gee, Pop, how could Motley
have stolen the Volkswagen?
His arm and leg were in a cast.
He couldn't shift gears or use
the clutch pedal!

Birmingham:
That's right, Charlie.

2

Charlie Chan:

Number One son and honourable
Inspector forget very
important fact. Volkswagen in
question very easy to drive.

No. 1 son:
I don't get you, Pop.
Charlie Chan:
Let me explain.   (Ripple dissolve)

3

On night of crime, Motley
steal Volkswagen with automatic
stick shift transmission.
Volkswagen with automatic stick
shift have no clutch pedal.
So Motley not need left leg.

4

Volkswagen with automatic
stick shift can be driven
all over city without shifting.
So Motley not need right arm.

In conclusion only evil
man like Motley really need
is far better alibi.

Charlie Chan

Think Small

There are a lot of good cars you can get for $3400. This is two of them.

If you don't happen to need two cars, there's only one thing that you need less. One car that costs as much as two cars.

Unless you want to pay a lot of money for a lot of horsepower that you'll never use. There's only one state in the country where you can go faster than a Volkswagen — Nevada. (No speed limit — they're big gamblers out there.) The only extra horsepower you really need is for all those power gadgets. Which you need to drive a car that size. Which has to be that size to hold all those horses.

All of which also makes the average car cost almost as much to run as two Volkswagens. Considering a VW gets about 27 miles to a gallon of gas and about 40,000 miles to a set of tires.

But if you're still not sold on two bugs for the price of one beast, take advantage of this special introductory offer: one Volkswagen for half the price of two.

Live below your means.

If you'd like to get around the high cost of living, we have a suggestion:

Cut down on the high cost of getting around.

And buy a Volkswagen. It's only $1699*.

That's around $1200 less than the average amount paid for a new car today. (Leave it in the bank. More's coming.)

A VW saves you hundreds of dollars on upkeep over the years.

It takes pints, not quarts, of oil.

Not one iota of antifreeze.

And it gets about 27 miles to the gallon. The average car (thirsty devil that it is) only gets 14.

So the more you drive, the more you save.

And chances are, you'll drive it for years and years. (Since we never change the style, a VW never goes out of style.)

Of course, a VW's not much to look at. So a lot of people buy a big flashy car just to save face.

Try putting that in the bank.

All for the price of a fancier priced car.

$3260 is the latest average price paid for a new car these days. (So says the Automobile Manufacturers Association.) $3260 will also buy you a new range, a new refrigerator, a new dryer, a new washer, two new television sets, a record player and a $1639* Volkswagen.

Of course our little package doesn't include all those tricky little items you find on those fancier-priced cars. (Like electric ashtray cleaners. Or headlights that disappear when the sun comes out.)

But it does include good food, clean clothes, nice music and a chance to watch all the summer reruns in color.

A lot of people frown on a Volkswagen because they feel it doesn't offer enough in the way of fancy gadgetry.

Look again.

How fancy can you get?

There's a bit of the beast in every bug.

It doesn't take much to unleash the savage fury of a Volkswagen.

Take almost any old VW, replace the body, make a few simple adjustments, and you've got a Formula Vee racer.

How can a mild-mannered, practical, everyday Volkswagen convert so easily into something so delightfully impractical? In the words of the Formula Vee International Manual: "Volkswagen components seem to have been made expressly for use in a racing car."

"The engine, air-cooled and mostly aluminum, is light for its power output and already adapted to the rear-engine concept of modern racing cars."

"Its rugged construction provides a power plant which seems to be practically indestructible, even at racing speeds."

"Operating costs are amazingly low.

One set of tires will ordinarily last more than a season and one oil change a year is sufficient."

It seems that the same things that make the VW a sensible car for people who aren't in any particular hurry to get somewhere also make the Formula Vee a sensible car for people who are in a big hurry to get nowhere.

It does all the work,
but on Saturday night which one goes to the party?

Once upon a time there was an ugly little bug. It could go about 27 miles on just one gallon of gas. It could go about 40,000 miles on just one set of tires. And it could park in tiny little crevices no bigger than a bug. It was just right for taking father to the train or the children to school. Or for taking mother to the grocery store, drugstore, dime store and all the other enchanting places that mothers go when everyone else is working.

The ugly little bug was just like one of the family. But alas, it wasn't beautiful.

So for any important occasion the ugly little bug would be replaced. By a big beautiful chariot, drawn by 300 horses!

Then after a time, a curious thing happened. The ugly little bug (which was made very sturdily) never got uglier. But the big beautiful chariot didn't exactly get more beautiful.

In fact, in a few years its beauty began to fade. Until, lo and behold, the ugly little bug didn't look as ugly as the big beautiful chariot!

The moral being: if you want to show you've gotten somewhere, get a big beautiful chariot. But if you simply want to get somewhere, get a bug.

With 34 wives, even a king has to cut a few corners.

Big, fast, expensive cars have always been a passion with royalty. But a family man like King Njiiri of Kenya probably doesn't have very much passion to spare.

Or very much money. (Things have been kind of slow lately in the king business.) Which makes him the kind of king that a Volkswagen is really fit for.

The price of a brand new one—$1639*

—isn't much higher than the price of a brand new wife. And a VW is a lot cheaper to support.

It goes about 27 miles on a gallon of gas. About 40,000 miles on a set of tires.

A Volkswagen also comes apart very easily. It only takes about twenty minutes to take off a fender, or 45 minutes to take out the whole engine.) That makes repairing it

easy. And quite inexpensive.

But when it's not being taken apart, a VW holds together very nicely. So even though old ones cost a good deal, they're still a good deal.

Especially if you happen to get one that was owned by an elderly king who only used it to go to court.

BY APPOINTMENT TO HIS MAJESTY, KING NJIIRI

If you're not convinced the VW is an economical car, talk to some of the people who are losing a fortune on it.

Robert A. Walker
WALKER'S GULF GAS STATION
1421 Gervais Street
Columbia, South Carolina

Ronald M. Finnell
BOB'S AUTO SERVICE INC.
"Anti-freeze, tire chains and towing our specialty"
2820 South Elati Street
Englewood, Colorado

Jerry Goldfine
SAM'S AUTO REPAIRS
215 Avenue C
New York, New York

John Sheehan
JOHN SHEEHAN RECAPPING INC.
599 John Street
Bridgeport, Connecticut

Jerry T. Fuller
SUPERIOR TIRE COMPANY
530 Gervais Street
Columbia, South Carolina

Sal De Palma
DE PALMA BROTHERS
AUTO WRECKING CO.
Avenue C and Murray
Newark, New Jersey

Clyde H. Goddard
CLYDE TIRE COMPANY
12928 South Western Avenue
Gardena, California

Chuck Evan
CHUCK EVAN'S GAS & SERVICE
1600 Noblestown Rd.
Pittsburgh 5, Pa.

Robert Lagana
CHAMPION AUTO ENGINEERING
EXPERT RADIATOR REPAIRS
151 Brook Street
Eastchester, N.Y.

Don Farquhar
HOLLYWOOD TIRE COMPANY
1219 North Vine Street
Hollywood, California

Paul Tatsui
ABCO TRANSMISSION
3940 East Olympic Boulevard
Los Angeles, California

Sam Madwatkins
MATTY'S AUTO PARTS, INC.
543 West 35th Street
New York, New York

Earl C. Aeverman
DENVER ENGINE & TRANSMISSION
EXCHANGE INC.
7015 W. 36th Ave.
Wheat Ridge, Colorado

Thomas K. Cook
TOM'S AUTO SERVICENTER
977 East 21st South
Salt Lake City, Utah

At night, it's a moonroof.

For XX* extra dollars you can buy a Volkswagen with a hole in its roof.

As a matter of fact, 390 square inches of hole in the roof.

The VW sunroof, or moonroof, gives you enough space to get a full view of the Milky Way or the moon. (It's also perfect for satellite searching or counting stars.)

If you only want a three-quarter view of what's above, all you have to do is crank the crank a few turns to the left, and you have three-quarters of a hole in the roof.

A few more turns to the left and you've got an airtight, all steel roof overhead. It's padded and lined like the rest of the car so you can hardly tell it's there.)

A Volkswagen with a hole in its top is just as cheap to run as any other Volkswagen. (You won't have to moonlight at a second job to afford to run one.)

It'll go about 27 miles on a gallon of gas, and about 40,000 miles on a set of tires.

And you don't have to spend a tidy sum getting your car ready for winter. (It won't need snow tires or chains either.)

In short, this Volkswagen does just about everything any other Volkswagen does, plus a little more.

So you see, you don't have to have a hole in your head to buy a Volkswagen with a hole in its head.

It finally knows how to treat a lady.

A woman once said she'd prefer doing 10 loads of wash to driving a Volkswagen round the block.

What a few others said is unprintable. We got the message.

That's why you can now get a Volkswagen with something called an automatic

stick shift.*

It does away with a clutch pedal. (So your left foot is free to do whatever left feet do in cars.)

And it does away with shifting every other mile. (You merely shift once when you start out. Then once again when you

go over 55 mph.)

And no matter where you go, you'll get about 25 miles to a gallon of gas.

After all, what good is a car that's easy to drive.

If you can't afford to go any place.

Pick the right day to test drive a VW and you'll have the road to yourself.

Back when the weather was good, everybody was inviting you to come in and test drive their new whatevers.

But now that the weather isn't so good (and a test drive is really a test), the invitations have dropped off sharply.

Now maybe you can spare a little time to try out the new Volkswagen.

Not right this minute. Wait for a nice lousy day. The next time it's snowing or slushing or something like that, drive down to your VW dealer. (If you can make it in your car.)

He'll be happy to take you out and show you how a Volkswagen works when hardly anything else does.

How the weight of the motor on the rear wheels makes the VW dig in and go, in the snow or the mud, or even on ice.

As you pass all the stranded cars that passed their test drives in balmier days, he'll tell you about the VW's other cold-weather comforts.

The air-cooled motor. It doesn't freeze over, so it doesn't need anti-freeze or a winter thermostat.

And if you have to leave the car out on a cold wet night, it's got four coats of paint and a sealed bottom to keep it cozy.

 You've even got an edge with a Volkswagen if the worst happens and you get stuck.

What could be easier to push?

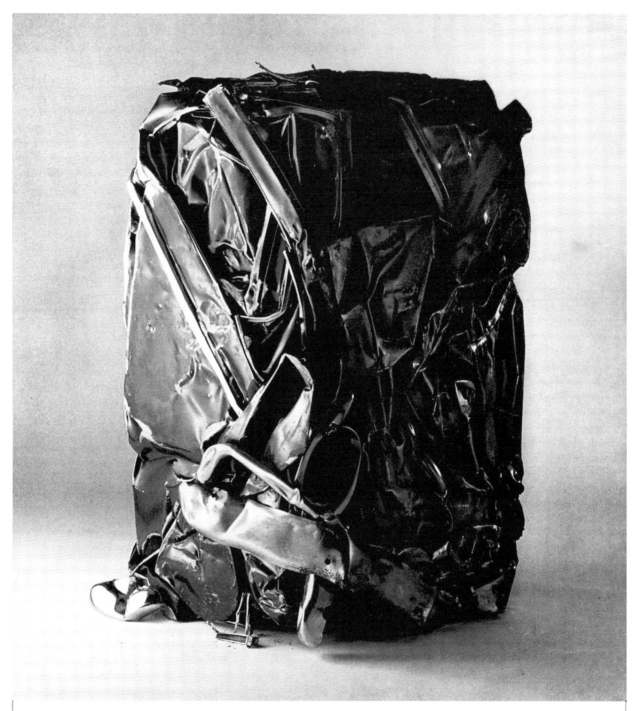

Every now and then a VW runs into a little trouble at the factory.

That hunk of junk was well on its way to being a Volkswagen, when it ran into a stone wall: a bunch of hard-nosed inspectors who pull enough parts off the line every day to make the equivalent of 20 cars. Or 2 freight cars full of scrap.

There are thousands of inspectors who literally pick every Volkswagen to pieces, every step of the way.

If there's a little scratch in a fender, it gets scratched. If there's a little nick in a bumper, it gets bumped.

Wherever ten people are doing something, there's an inspector to undo it. For the paint job alone, no less than 8 inspectors check every VW.

All that inspection doesn't mean the work isn't done carefully. The men who make the VW make it very well. The inspectors just make it perfect.

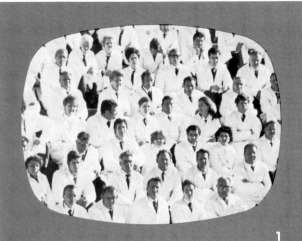

1

Open on Roman Ampitheatre filled
with rows of white coated VW
inspectors.

Dramatic VO:

Welcome to the Volkswagen
factory where every day a blood
thirsty mob of 8,397 inspectors
decrees whether or not a
Volkswagen will live. Or die.

2

Should it lose favour with any
one of them...
even for the slightest whim,
it will die.

3

Should any one of its 5,000
parts be deemed defective
even for reasons unseen by the
untrained eye, it will die.

4

For only after every single
part has passed at least three
inspections. And only after
16,000 triumphant inspections
in all, may a contestant then
leave this arena with the
worthy title: "Volkswagen"

Now let the games begin.

SFX: Drums roll, crowd rises
      to their feet.

Coliseum

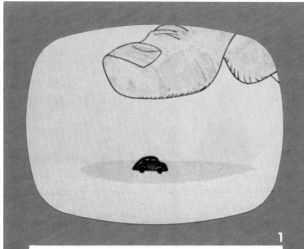

1

Open on animated VW car 'buzzing' across frame.

The Beetle may look harmless to you but a lot of people are afraid of it.

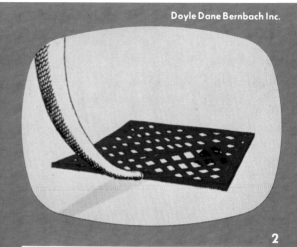

2

Ford is trying to squash it in their commercials.

Chrysler is taking swats at it too.

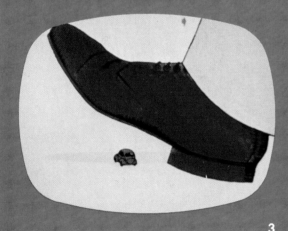

3

GM would like to exterminate it.
And even American motors is doing its best to stamp it out.

THE VOLKSWAGEN BEETLE

4

They must be very, very jealous of the Beetle.

Why else would it bother them so much.

Fly Swatter

1

Open on funeral procession
of limousines each containing
the benefactors of a will.

MVO:

I, Maxwell E. Snavely, being
of sound mind and body do
bequeath the following:

2

To my wife Rose, who spent
money like there was no
tomorrow, I leave $100 and a
calendar...
To my sons Rodney and Victor,
who spent every dime I ever
gave them on fancy cars and
fast women....

I leave $50 in dimes...

3

To my business partner, Jules,
who's motto was "spend, spend,
spend" I leave nothing, nothing,
nothing.

And to my other friends and
relatives who also never learned
the value of a dollar, I leave...
a dollar.

4

Finally, to my nephew, Harold,
who oft time said:

"A penny saved is a penny
earned". And who also oft
time said "Gee Uncle Max, it
sure pays to own a Volkswagen".

I leave my entire fortune of
one hundred billion dollars.

Funeral

Doyle Dane Bernbach Inc.

1

Open on futuristic archeologists
in a barren landscape.

MVO:
The Place, the desert.
The year, 2270.

2

Who knows 300 years from now
someone may find a 1970
Vokswagen still running.

Because the 1970 VW has a new
longer lasting engine.

3

Driver: Thanks.

MVO:
The 1970 VW engine is bigger,
more powerful, yet weighs the
same as our old engine. So it
doesn't have to work as hard.

4

The way we figure it will last
longer than any other VW engine.
How much longer?
Who knows.

Archaeologists

It takes a week to make the car. And 3 years to make the mechanic.

Oh the difference between a bug and a man.

In just seven days a piece of steel evolves into a sturdy Volkswagen.

But only after three years does a raw recruit evolve into a bona fide Volkswagen mechanic.

It's not an easy process.

He starts with a lowly doorknob and works his way up to the electrical system. (With an eagle-eyed supervisor over his shoulder.)

He takes every part apart. And puts it back together again. Over and over and over.

Then we clock him.

If he does the right job in the right time, bully for him.

He does it again.

Only after he passes the test twice do we feel he's mastered that part. And can go on to another.

But this is only part of the grind.

When this man's not working on the VW, we're working on him. At a Volkswagen training school.

There he spends seven hours a day in class studying about the car.

So by the end of his apprenticeship, he knows every nook and cranny in a VW.

For once, man counts as much as the machine.

Who in the world seals the bottom? Volkswagen.

Here's a side of the Volkswagen that very few people know about: the underside.

It is not only enclosed, but sealed with rubber to make it practically airtight. So tight we get persistent reports it will even float.

But here's a more useful advantage: a VW sloshes through water that brings most traffic to a standstill.

Notice how flat and smooth the VW bottom is. No hollow pockets and hanging parts to trap air and slow you down. Less drag, better gas mileage.

On most cars, control wires and cables are left exposed. But you don't see wires under a VW; all you see is the steel bottom that protects them.

A Volkswagen depreciates less than any other car because less can happen to it. Its shape remains the same. Its works intact.

The Volkswagen's built-in heater and defroster are part of the body—designed into the car and therefore included in the price. $1,675.* top to bottom.

Why is our nose so stubby?

The VW doesn't need a long front hood because the engine's in back of the car.

This gives you a couple of advantages over the long-nosed jobs.

Obviously, it makes for a sturdier car. So you can move in and out of traffic. And in and out of tight little parking spots.

Your chances of denting a fender in the process are practically nil, too. Because the VW's short hood lets you look right down your nose at the road.

The good is this: Everything on the VW is there for a reason. Including our changes.

Unless you've nosed around VWs for years, you may not be aware of things like our fully synchromesh transmission.

Or our quieter, more powerful engine.

On our 3,012 other working improvements.

On the face of it, the VW looks the same, underneath, it's changed.

Which is one reason the VW depreciates so little and stays in style year after year.

Nose and all.

Every new one comes slightly used.

The road to becoming a Volkswagen is a rough one. The obstacles are many.

Some make it.

Some crack.

Those who make it are scrutinized by 8,397 inspectors. 1807 of whom are finicky women.)

They're subjected to 16,000 different inspections.

They're driven the equivalent of 3 miles on a special test stand.

Every engine is broken in.

Every transmission.

Many bugs are then plucked from the production line. Their sole function in life is to be tested and not to be sold.

We put them through water to make sure they don't leak.

We put them through mud and salt to make sure they won't rust.

They climb hills to test handbrakes and clutches.

Then comes the dreaded wind tunnel and a trip over 8 different road surfaces to check out the ride.

Torsion bars are twisted 100,000 times to make sure they torsion properly.

Keys are turned on 25,000 times to make sure they don't break off in keylocks.

And so it goes on.

200 Volkswagens are rejected every day.

It's a tough league.

They don't make them like they used to.

They may still look like they used to, but that doesn't mean we still make them that way.

We used to have a tiny rear window. Now there's a big one.

We used to have a plain old rear seat. Now there's one that folds down.

Over the years, engine power has been increased by 76%.

A dual brake system has been added.

The heater is much improved.

Fact is, over the years, over 2,200 such improvements have been made. Yet, you have to be some sort of a car nut to tell a new one from an old one.

Which, of course, was the plan.

In 1949, when we decided not to out-date the bug, some of the big auto names making big, fancy changes were Kaiser, Hudson and Nash.

Not that we were right and they were wrong, but one thing's for sure: They don't make them like they used to either.

The best kept secret in Washington, D.C.

What's the most popular car among diplomats in Washington, D.C.?

Put that question to a diplomat and you get a very diplomatic answer.

In other words, they don't tell.

So we did some snooping around on our own and contrary to public opinion, the car most diplomats buy is neither very big nor very fancy nor very impressive.

Hint: It can be bought and serviced in 140 countries throughout the world.

Hint: It costs $1749* in the U.S.A.

Hint: It has tremendous resale value.

Final hint: It gets around 27 miles to the gallon and uses no antifreeze whatsoever.

At last count, there were over 1200 diplomats and embassy staff members driving this little car throughout Washington.

So that story about big important people driving only big, important-looking cars may not be altogether true.

On the other hand, if big important people would rather have you believe they drive only big, important-looking cars, that's all right with us.

We won't let the bug out of the bag.

It's been from New York to L.A. without moving an inch.

Another miracle from Volkswagen:

A Volkswagen goes through one of its most grueling tests in a gigantic wind tunnel.

Once inside, it can take (in effect) a trip between any two given cities.

We calculate beforehand what the road, altitude, weather and speed would actually be.

Then we reproduce these same conditions inside the wind tunnel.

This way we find out (before you do) what a Volkswagen can take on the road. And what it can't take.

And anything big it can't take, we do something about.

So if you and a Volkswagen ever hit high winds in Miami or Chicago or even Anchorage, Alaska, you have one reassuring thought:

A VW's probably been through it before.

Sometimes we get the feeling we're being followed.

Everybody's getting into the act.

Everybody's making a small car.

And since we've made more of them than anyone else, we thought we'd pass along some things we've learned about the business over the years.

First off, there's no doubt about it, the only way to make an economy car is expensively.

So Rule No. 1, don't scrimp.

Get yourself the best possible engineers in the business and then hire 9,000 or so top inspectors to keep them on their toes.

Next, try to develop an engine that's not a gas-guzzler. If you can get it to run on pints of oil instead of quarts, great. If you can get it to run on air instead of water, fantastic.

Work on things to make your car last longer. Like giving it 45 pounds of paint to protect its top and a full-length steel bottom to protect its bottom.

Important: Make sure you can service any year car you make. There's nothing worse than having someone find out that a part they need to make their car go is no longer on hand or on top.

Finally, spend less time worrying about what your new car looks like and more time worrying about how it works.

Perfecting a good economy car is a time-consuming business.

So far it has consumed 25 years of our time.

After a few years, it starts to look beautiful.

"Ugly, isn't it?"

"No class."

"Looks like an afterthought."

"Good for laughs."

"Stubby buggy."

"El Pig-O."

New York Magazine said: "And then there is the VW, which retains its value better than anything else. A 1956 VW is worth more today than any American sedan built the same year, with the possible exception of a Cadillac."

Around 27 miles to the gallon. Pints of oil instead of quarts. No radiator.

Rear engine traction.

Low insurance.

$1,799* is the price.

Beautiful, isn't it?

Who knows what evil lurks in the hearts of used cars?

DOYLE DANE BERNBACH INC. ADVERTISING B

NEW YORK, N. Y. 10036 LO 4-1234

RADIO · TELEVISION

program		air date	
client	VOLKSWAGEN	length	
product		job no.	

(sound: motorcycle pulling to a stop)

Policeman: You the fellow phoned in the report, oldtimer?

Oldtimer: That's right. There's the critter I told you about.

Policeman: What critter?

Oldtimer: Right there! What's the matter with you?

Policeman: Well that's a Volkswagen.

Oldtimer: I don't care what you call it, it should'nt be running around loose. I've been trailing it through the desert for days.

Policeman: Just who are you?

Oldtimer: Name's Esert Bush, been prospecting for uranium.

Policeman: And how long you been up in those mountains?

Oldtimer: Oh, about 25 years I reckon...wouldn't come out now if I hadn't spotted that there, ah...

Policeman: Volkswagen.

Oldtimer: Yeah, well see, I come on it grazing outside that there motel. I was sneaking up when this fellow comes out, opens up its face and feeds it.

Policeman: Feeds it?

Oldtimer: Yep. Two suitcase and a bag of golf sticks. Darndest thing I ever seen.

Policeman : Mr Bush, the Volkswagen is a car!

Oldtimer: Are you loco? Why that thing run across the desert for hours and never stopped for gas or water...that's how come I kept losing it.

Policeman: Well, it doesn't use water...and very little gas or oil for that matter.

Oldtimer: Well, I'll be. I oughta get me one of them for hauling uranium.

Policeman: Hey, did you strike it rich up there?

Oldtimer: Maybe I did, maybe I didn't. Wouldn't tell you anyway Officer.

Policeman: why not?

Oldtimer: You got beady eyes.

We finally came up with a beautiful picture of a Volkswagen.

A Volkswagen starts looking good when everything else starts looking bad.

Let's say it's late at night and you can't sleep. It's 10 below and you forgot to put antifreeze in your car.

(A Volkswagen doesn't use antifreeze. Its engine is cooled by air.)

Let's say it's now morning: You start your car and the gas gauge reads Empty.

(Even with a gallon left, you should go approximately 27 miles in a VW.)

Let's say you notice on your way out of the driveway that every other car on your block is stuck in the snow.

(A VW goes very well in snow because the engine is in the back. It gives the rear wheels much better traction.)

Let's say you make it into town and the only parking space is half a space between a snow plow and a big, fat wall.

(A VW is small enough to fit into half a parking space.)

Let's say it's now 9:15 a.m. and the only other guy in the office is your boss.

(Now what could be more beautiful than that?)

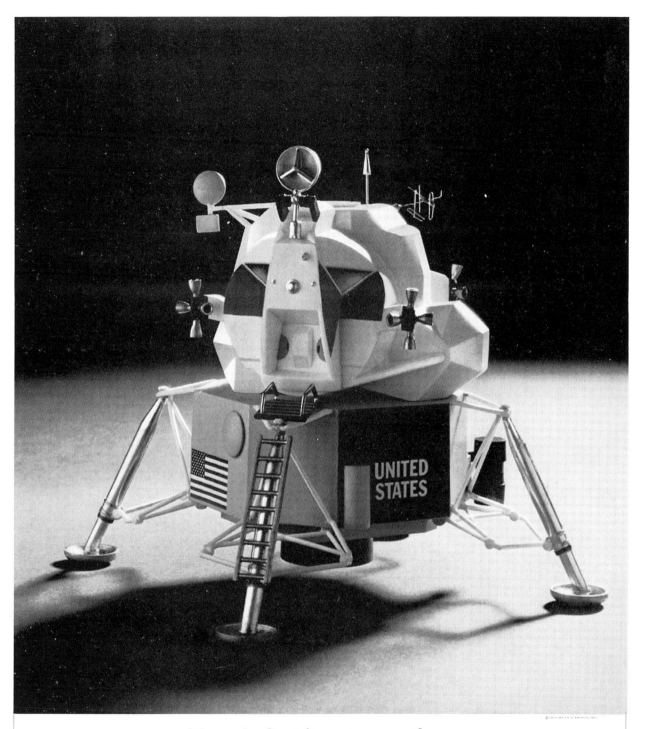

It's ugly, but it gets you there.

Doyle Dane Bernbach Inc.

1

Open on spacecraft approaching planet.

<u>MVO</u>: As any scientist can tell you, travelling to an unknown planet is not that much of a problem anymore.

2

The problem is getting around when you get up there.

First off, since nobody likes to run out of gas or oil in strange places, you need a vehicle that won't use too much gas or oil.

3

You need a vehicle that won't boil over on hot, unknown planets.

Or freeze up on cold ones.

And since surface conditions can run anywhere from green cheese to molasses you need a vehicle with exceptional traction.

4

All of which is why, we the crew of the V-1500 chose the Volkswagen Sedan.

The best car on Zeno.

Moonshot

In Honduras, gasoline costs 52¢ a gallon.

And temperatures soar to 120 above. And water is scarce. And roads are wicked. And people aren't rich. So is it any wonder that in a town like San Pedro Sula, Honduras, 100% of the taxis are Volkswagen taxis? And 100% of the buses are Volkswagen buses?

1799 dólares.*

27 millas por galón. No agua. A Volkswagen makes as much sense in Spanish as it does in English.

Doyle Dane Bernbach Inc.

Open on announcer standing in front of curtains on stage.

Anncr: Presenting the Great Zandu.

SFX: Fanfare.

Anncr: The great Zandu will now amaze you with his incredible mental powers.

Zandu levitates VW on stage.

SFX: Oohs and ahs of the audience.

Car falls through floor:

MVO: When a car is essential to your job. . . you want it fixed in a hurry.

A Volkswagen dealer can replace an engine in little over an hour. Or a fender with just ten bolts.

And with genuine Volkswagen parts always available, you'll be back to work in no time.

Anncr: Ladies and gentlemen, presenting the Great Zandu. The great Zandu will now. . .

Cut back to curtains as they reveal fully repaired VW and partially repaired Zandu.

Zandu

Doyle Dane Bernbach Inc.

1

Open on two identical houses.

VO: Mr. Jones and Mr. Krempler
were neighbours. They each had
$3,000.

2

With his money Mr. Jones bought
himself a $3,000 car.

With his money Mr. Krempler
bought himself......

3

... a new refrigerator. . .
... a new range. . .
... a new washer. . .
... a new dryer. . .
... a record player. . . .
... two new television sets . .
... and a brand new Volkswagen.

4

Now Mr. Jones is faced with
that age old problem. . . .

Keeping up with the Krempler's.

Jones and Krempler

1

Open on two farmhands by barn door.

Dumb old Barney: You gonna tell me about the rabbits again, George?

George: No Barney, you know what we have to do today.

DOB: Yeah, I remember George. But I can't drive no Volkswagen. I can't work no gear shift. I can't use no clutch pedal.

2

George: Barney, if I've told you once now, I've told you a hundred times. This is a new thing Volkswagen has. It's called the automative stick shift. There ain't no clutch pedal, and there ain't no problems.

DOB: I don't know George; I just don't know.

3

George: Barney, you get in the car.

DOB: I get in the car.

George: You turn on the key.

DOB: I turn on the key.

George: You put it in drive.

DOB: I put it in drive.

4

George: And you drive away.

DOB: And I drive away.

George: That's it Barney, it's as simple as A,B,C.

DOB: That's right George, it's as simple as ah. . .Ah. . . uh. . . uh.

Barney and George

1

Open on man entering songwriter's office.

Man: Good afternoon, gentlemen I'm from Volkswagen and I've got a music problem.

Ronnie & Johnnie (singing) I'm Ronnie, I'm Johnnie. You got a problem. We got a song.

Man: Well, we're very excited about the 29 improvements in our 1972 Super Beetle.

Doyle Dane Bernbach Inc.

2

I thought perhaps, a theme song..

Johnnie: We do car gigs.

Ronnie: Yeah. . .

Man: Improvement Number One, the compression ratio has been optimised through dish pistons. .

1972 SUPER BEETLE

3

Ronnie and Johnnie (singing) Dish pistons optimised compression ratio. . . .

Got anything else?

Man: Improvement Number Two, increased air inlet groupings. (Dissolve) Number eighteen an advanced manifold pre-heating system. (Dissolve)

4

Finally, improvement Number 29, floating bearing for most mounting points. The most improved Volkswagen ever.

Ronnie: Kid, five thousand canaries whistling the Bluebird of Happiness couldn't help you.

Ronnie and Johnnie

September 4, 1968

Volkswagen of America
Englewood Cliffs
New Jersey

Dear Sir:

After seeing your unusual and off-beat advertisement of Volkswagens, it seems that we own one that may be of interest to you.

Below are the facts about our Volkswagen:

Purchased: ~~DePaul~~ De Paul Motors,
            Gadsden, Ala., 1961
Model: 1959
Mileage: 605,798 (only two engine changes)
Travels: Over 800 miles per day
         5 days per week.

Thank you;

Sincerely,
Mrs. Carson Brooks
210 East 4th St.
Oxford, Ala.

We'd like to thank Mrs. Brooks for allowing us to re-print her exceptional story in its entirety © Volkswagen of America, Inc.

After 30 Volkswagens, Father Bittman still believes.

In the beginning, Father Aloysius Bittman bought a bug.

That was in 1957 when he joined the staff of St. Anthony's Indian Mission in Mandaree, North Dakota.

Since then, Father Bittman has gone a long way. In 30 Volkswagens.

Owning two or three at a time, the Bittman staff travels 600 miles per week in each. Over dirt and gravel roads and in temperatures that have been known to go to 55 below.

A couple of Volkswagens ago, Father Bittman's '65 broke through the Garrison Reservoir ice.

"It was a good time for praying," he said.

Luckily, one 255 pound priest and one 1808 pound bug floated to safety. After the ice was chopped away and a quick oil change, the good father and his faithful companion were on their way.

He was a bit peeved about the oil change though.

"It set the Mission back $1.80," complained Father Aloysius Bittman.

The 1970 VW will stay ugly longer.

What hath Volkswagen wrought this year?

A longer-lasting engine, that's what.

It's more powerful than the old engine. (Top speed. 81 mph vs. 78 mph.)

It has better acceleration.

But most important, it doesn't have to work as hard to get you where you're going.

Thus, according to every calculation known to man, it will last even longer.

And just to make sure the engine and every other VW part leads a long, happy life, we have another surprise for 1970:

The Volkswagen Diagnostic Checkup.

Now before the name scares you away, listen to what it is:

VW Diagnosis is an exclusive free service checkup by trained technicians using special diagnostic equipment.

The equipment is faster and more thorough than any mechanic alive.

And it's so advanced, it can actually tell you you have a problem early, before it becomes a real problem.

When you buy a new VW, you're entitled to four of these checkups free.

Of course if a problem due to defective workmanship at the factory is spotted during the first 24 months or 24,000 miles (whichever comes first), we'll end up footing the bill. Not you.

During this period, when we do make these repairs free, the parts will be free, the labor will be free, the diagnostic checkups will be free.

What could be a better deal than that?

You buy a bug.

We take care of the bugs.

Is somebody learning how to fix Volkswagens on your Volkswagen?

Anybody can put up a sign that says, "We fix Volkswagens."

But just because somebody can spell Volkswagen doesn't mean he can fix one.

VW fixing is an education unto itself.

Only there's no Volkswagen School.

There's a VW engine school.

A VW transmission school.

An electrical school. And so on and on.

The survivors of Volkswagen training schools are as much engineers as mechanics.

They know all there is to know about Volkswagens. Or else.

And so behind every genuine VW replacement part stands a calm VW dealer.

If something goes wrong—boom. Out it comes and in goes another one.

No problem.

All this is part of the quaint VW notion that the service has got to be as good as the car itself.

If it isn't, we're dead. And we know it.

So our people learn at our expense, grate on our nerves, and practice on our cars.

Not yours.

We don't have to start from scratch each year.

We've been making the same basic VW for so long now, you'd think we'd be bored with the whole thing.

But the fact is, we're still learning.

For no matter how perfect we think one year's model is, there's always an engineer who wants to make it more perfect.

You see, at the Volkswagen factory we spend 100% of our time making our car work better and 0% making it look better.

Any change is an improvement.

And when we do make new parts we try to make them fit older models. So there's nothing to stop a Volkswagen from running forever.

(Which may explain why Volkswagens are worth so much at trade-in time.)

Starting from scratch each year can get in the way of all that.

Just when they've ironed out the kinks in the current model, they have to face the kinks in the next.

We'll never understand all the hoopla over the "big changes" for next year's models.

Weren't they proud of this year's?

49 TUCKER · 49 PACKARD · 49 DE SOTO · 49 STUDEBAKER · 49 VOLKSWAGEN · 49 HUDSON

Where are they now?

Return with us now to those wondrous days of yesteryear.

It's 1949 and automobiles are getting longer, lower and wilder.

Massive bumpers are a big hit. Fins are in. And everyone's promising to "keep in style with the times."

But then, times changed.

Massive bumpers and fins went out. So did every car shown above, except the VW.

You see, back in '49, when all those other guys were worrying about how to improve the way their cars looked, we were worrying about how to improve the way ours worked.

And you know what?

2,200 improvements later, we still worry about the same thing.

© VOLKSWAGEN OF AMERICA, INC.

A rare photo.

You don't see too many pictures like this because we really never pictured ourselves this way.

For the past 23 years, while just about every other car company has been feeling the pulse of the nation and changing the looks of their cars accordingly, we've been fixing the inside of our little car

just so you wouldn't have to have it fixed so often.

The result is that today, there's not one single part on a '71 Volkswagen that hasn't been improved at least once.

Recently, a top level executive from a big automotive firm summed up our position on the subject for us:

"Consumers today are more interested in quality, low cost of operation and durability, and less interested in styling, power and performance."

 That's top level thinking?

Our top level thinkers have been thinking that way since 1949.

One hour later, it won't get hungry again.

If you need a car to make food deliveries with, doesn't it make sense to use one that won't eat up much profit?

It did to Mr. Chuck Lew, Chinese restaurateur, White Plains, New York.

His honorable Volkswagen has been delivering everything from wonton soup to leechee nuts for close to two years.

All the while averaging 25 miles to a gallon of gas, using pints of oil instead of quarts, and no water or antifreeze.

Since it can't boil over or freeze under, the egg foo gets wherever it's going while it's still young.

Since we never change the way the car looks, spare parts are as readily available from his Volkswagen dealer as are spare ribs from his restaurant.

And since Mr. Lew charges a 50c delivery fee and uses a car that costs roughly one-fourth of that for the average trip, he'd be crazy to trade it in.

Even for all the tea in China.

Before you look at their new ones, look at their old ones.

Now that new car time is upon us, gosh knows, we hate to be the ones to spoil all the fun.

After all, what's more exciting than taking the family down to see the shiny new models or to hear the fast-talking salesmen, or maybe even to pick up a free balloon?

It's just that during all that hoopla and razzle-dazzle, you may not want to pick up one of those exciting new cars.

For the unpleasant fact of the matter is that junkyards throughout the country are doing a thriving business on automobiles that seemingly just yesterday were showroom stars.

Which is why we suggest a trip to the junkyard before you decide to put a new car in your own yard.

And why we suggest that that new car be a Volkswagen. For while we can't promise you how long one will last, we can tell you that over 13 million Volkswagens are still on the road.

And when one drops out, even then it's not always destined to be dropped in a pile. For old Volkswagens have a habit of becoming other things: Like new dune buggys.

All in all, we owe it all to a decision we made 24 years ago.

To spend very little time making our little car look better. And a great deal of time making it work better.

So far, that one decision has kept us out of a lot of trouble.

The $35,000 Volkswagen.

Have we gone stark raving mad?

No, but when we heard this car was on display at the Los Angeles International Auto Show, we thought somebody had.

As it turned out, there was a method to the owner's madness.

Why not transform the world's best known economy car into the world's most economical limousine?

After all, a lot of the things that make great luxury cars great are already there in the humble little Bug.

Like 23 years of perfecting every single part of the car.

And subjecting it to over 16,000 different inspections before we sell it to you.

And having it worth lots of money to you, when you sell it to someone else.

So why not stretch it out to limo length?

Why not add an intercom, bar and mahogany woodwork and tufted English upholstery and a carriage lamp to signal the doorman?

Why not be the savingest millionaire on the road?

That, children, is exactly how the rich get richer.

A common misconception about air-conditioning old Volkswagens.

If you've been driving around in the summer secretly jealous of your Volkswagen's air-cooled engine, consider this an invitation.

To come in and have an air conditioner installed.

Myths about Volkswagen air conditioning to the contrary, it won't be a big, bulky apparatus that takes away your legroom.

And it won't be a super-powerful unit that takes away your breath.

Rather, it's an air conditioner that's especially made for each type of VW.

So if you own a Karmann Ghia or a Beetle, it will be just right.

If it's our 411, Squareback Sedan, or Type 3, it will be fine.

And if it's our big Station Wagon, it will be enough to cool you off without turning it into an ice-Box.

Doyle Dane Bernbach Inc.

1

2

Open on stand at forties' car show.

Male Presenter: And now the star of the 1949 Auto Show. . . The car of the future. The car the public wants. The all new De Soto .

Lady Presenter: Just as long skirts will be the next look on the fashion scene, the Studebaker will be the next look on the automotive scene.

3

4

2nd Male Presenter: There's no doubt about it, next year every car in America will have holes in its side.

3rd Male Presenter: So the man to see if you're buying your next car for keeps, is your nearby Packard dealer.

Female Trio: Longer, lower, wider, the 49 Hudson is the car for you. . . .

VW Presenter: So Volkswagen will constantly be changing, impro- ving and refining this car. Not necessarily to keep in style with the times, but to make a better car. Which means to all of you. . . better mileage. . .

MVO: Of all the promises made at the 1949 Auto Show we at Volkswagen kept ours.

49 Auto Show

$1845

Volkswagen Sedan 111. Suggested retail price, West Coast P.O.E.
Local taxes and other dealer delivery charges, if any, additional.

1

Open on still of VW Beetle
with price underneath.

MVO: You have exactly 10 seconds
to memorize. . . . .

$1845

Volkswagen Sedan 111. Suggested retail price, West Coast P.O.E.
Local taxes and other dealer delivery charges, if any, additional.

2

The price of a 1971 Volkswagen
Beetle.

$1845

Volkswagen Sedan 111. Suggested retail price, West Coast P.O.E.
Local taxes and other dealer delivery charges, if any, additional.

3

$1845

Volkswagen Sedan 111. Suggested retail price, West Coast P.O.E.
Local taxes and other dealer delivery charges, if any, additional.

4

You may take notes.

Price

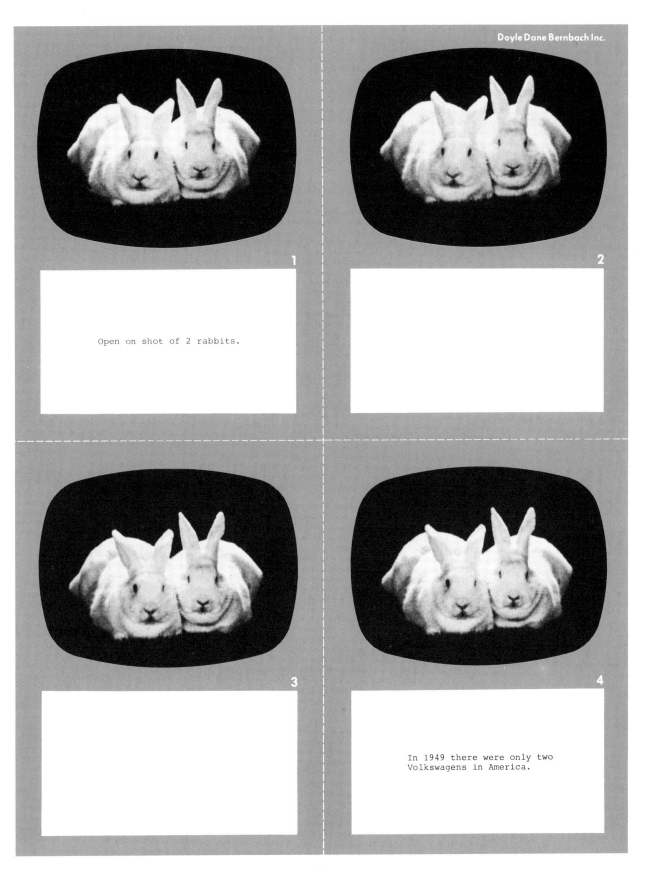

Rabbits

92

Doyle Dane Bernbach Inc.

1

Open on presenter standing between 2 VWs.

Presenter: Folks, trade in your old Volkswagen. . . .

2

On a brand new one.

3

4

Is this the new one?

Trade-In

A rational alternative to rationing gas.

What's right with this picture? Well if it were true, we'd be saving 26 billion, 560 million gallons of gas every year.

How did we arrive at that figure? Since we're a nation of national averages, we know the average car uses about 735 gallons of gas a year. The Beetle, 399*. Turn the eighty-five million average cars

on the road right now into Beetles, and it works out to a saving of 28,560,000,000 (give or take a few gallons).

Now we haven't figured out all the water and antifreeze that would be saved with the Beetle's air-cooled engine. Nor can we compute the extra parking space that would be around.

Not to mention all the money people would be able to save in a world of Volkswagens.

But we know for sure that this is no pipe dream. There already are police car Beetles up in Ossining. And a custom built, chauffeur-driven Bug in L. A. And Volkswagen taxis all over Honduras. And a

Beetle that herds cattle in Missouri.

So with gas prices going up and rationing becoming a reality, the Beetle never looked so good. In fact, you might almost call it beautiful.

Few things in life work as well as a Volkswagen.

Which man would you vote for?

We'll fix it so good it'll be hard to close.

1

Open on presenter standing by
winched up VW.

<u>Presenter</u>: Try looking at a
Volkswagen this way. It's the
only small car with a sealed
steel bottom. That leaves
nothing exposed beneath it.

2

It's the only small car with a
four-wheel independent suspension
system. And it's built to take
a little punishment.

3

As small as the VW is it's
covered with 13 pounds of paint.
Outside, and in. Even in places
you can't see but which
corrosion can find.

In fact the VW is so well put
together, it's practically
airtight.

4

Now, what other car gives you
this kind of quality at this
kind of price.

Splash

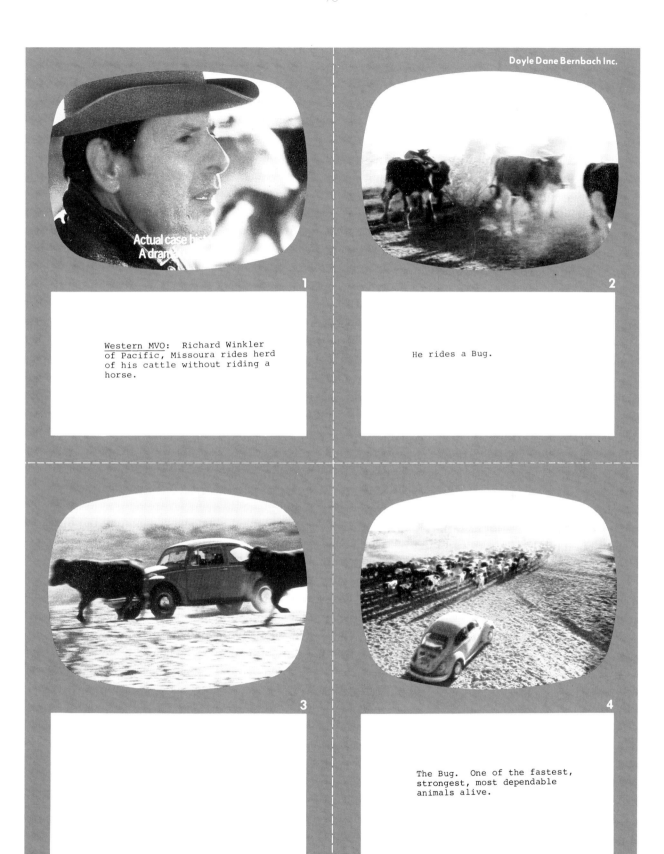

Round Up

Doyle Dane Bernbach Inc.

1

Open on mechanic approaching
mass of VW parts laid out on
floor.

MVO: Getting out of the
Volkswagen mechanic's school
isn't exactly easy.

Before our mechanic works on
your VW, our training instructors
work on him.

2

Until he can show us where every
bolt, every washer, every nut
goes, what every part does and
how to service every single one
of them.

3

It takes three years to make a
Volkswagen mechanic. So no
wonder there isn't anything he
can't do to any Volkswagen
ever made.

4

Instructor: Now, take it apart.

Student Mechanic

Can you still get prime quality for $1.26 a pound?

A pound of Volkswagen isn't cheap compared to other cars. But what you pay for is the quality. Prime quality.

Just look at what you get for your money:

13 pounds of paint, some of it in places you can't even see. (So you can leave a Volkswagen out overnight and it won't spoil.)

A watertight, airtight, sealed steel bottom that protects against rocks, rain, rust and rot.

Over 1,000 inspections per one Beetle.

1,014 inspectors who are so finicky that they reject parts you could easily ride around with and not even detect there was anything wrong.

Electronic Diagnosis that tells you what's right and wrong with important parts of your car.

A 1600 cc aluminum-magnesium engine that gets 25* miles to a gallon of regular gasoline.

Volkswagen's traditionally high resale value.

Over 22,000 changes and improvements on a car that was well built to begin with.

What with all the care we take in building every single Volkswagen, we'd like to call it a filet mignon of a car. Only one problem. It's too tough.

Few things in life work as well as a Volkswagen.

*DIN 70030

Practice makes perfect.

1949 1950 1951 1952 1953 1954 1955 1956 1957 1958 1959 1960 1961 1962 1963 1964 1965 1966 1967 1968 1969 1970

And practice we've had plenty.

Would you believe 12 million Volkswagens all over the world? Or 3½ million here in the U.S.A.?

Well, there are. And, in a way, every VW we make is a little better than the one we made before.

Because we don't wrench ourselves out of shape making fake improvements every 12 months. Instead, we make about 5,000 changes every year, that we don't even talk about. We simply do what needs doing to make the VW work better all the time. Not to look different all the time.

We are car makers, not metal benders.

So what have we got to show for 25 years?

Only the most highly developed car on the road.

Take any old Volkswagen from any old year. It will still be alright.

We never knew how to make it any other way, and we still don't. It still helps to open a window to close a door, even on an old one.

Take any new Volkswagen.

If there's a nick in the paint or a scratch on the chrome, somebody else put it there. Not us.

You won't find a jumble of wires under the dashboard. Just smooth, shiny, painted steel. Under the hood? Shiny and smooth. The glove compartment door? Shiny and smooth. Around the engine? Shiny and smooth.

Even if you removed the door panel, you'd find it the same. Smooth and shiny.

If you saw the way we made them, you'd know why this is true.

One in eight VW employees is an inspector. And the head inspector reports to the head of the company, not to the head salesman.

Only one other car maker in the world uses this system, and their prices start at $5,000.

Every wheel rim we turn out is inspected. 100% of them. Every brake drum. Every gas tank.

Every engine is run in before it becomes part of the car. And after.

Every single part that has to do with safety is individually inspected and then individually stamped with the inspector's individual initials.

(We also have inspectors who inspect inspectors. And until a man does it right, we don't let him put his trams on it.)

The Volkswagen paint shops are so clean and well-ventilated, our spray men don't even wear masks. If you do come to visit us, drop into the spray shop for a breath of fresh air.

Clean as the spray shops are, though, every car is still hand-sanded and hand-washed to make sure there isn't a speck of dust in or on or under the paint.

When a VW gets to the end of the line, an inspector checks to see that the engine, the electrical system, the brakes, and everything else that makes a VW stop and go puts out what we put in.

We make 5,000 cars a day; we check 5,000.

Speaking of testing, we have 2 test tracks that are literally Hell on wheels. With hills and valleys and hairpin turns and cobblestone stretches that simply aren't found on American roads.

Every change we make (or don't make) lives or dies on one of our tracks.

We also have the world's only computerized wind tunnel, big enough to test aerodynamic forces and climatic conditions. On real cars, not models.

So. Just because you've seen one VW, don't think you've seen them all.

By changing the way we change and testing the way we test, the Volkswagen we sell today is a whole other machine.

Over the years, we have practically doubled the VW's horsepower, but the engine should last even longer.

The luggage space in new VWs is far greater. The car is quieter and rides better. You can get a VW without a clutch pedal these days, and still get 25 miles to a gallon.

We've added thoughtful little things like a door pocket for the driver. Like tiny little wires that defrost the rear window electrically. Like a little pop-up shield to protect the dashboard when you slide out the ashtray.

And happily, we still sell it for a mere $1839.*

But when we take your $1839, we give you interest on your money by not losing interest in your car.

We are the only car people in the world with Medi-car, the Volkswagen Diagnosis System.

As part of our continuing madness, we give you 4 free top-to-bottom checkups with your new VW.

You just maintain your car according to the Volkswagen maintenance schedule. If any factory part is defective in material or workmanship, any U.S. or Canadian VW dealer will repair or replace it, within 24 months or 24,000 miles, whichever comes first. And he will do it free of charge.

In short, whatever Medi-car finds, that's covered by our guarantee gets fixed free.

Every last VW dealer has this electronic Medi-car equipment, and if you already own a VW, you can get the checkups for just a few dollars.

On that topic, if you do own an older Volkswagen (even a '49), and need a part, don't worry. You can drive into any VW dealer's and he won't laugh or even raise an eyebrow.

He will congratulate you and fix it.

Because most VW parts, changed though they may be, still fit most VWs.

With this instinct for survival, it's no wonder that Volkswagens are sold in 140 countries throughout the world.

It's no wonder that when civilization comes to a country, it usually comes in a Volkswagen.

And it's no wonder that half the people who buy VWs here in the United States are coming back for their second or fifth or eighth time.

We let other people make their cars bigger and smaller and taller and shorter.

We just go on making ours longer.

Is nothing sacred?

Here we've been slaving away for 25 years, improving the Volkswagen's insides, and letting the outside take care of itself.

And now—boom! People are trying to show us how it ought to be done.

"Why?" we asked.

"To make it look as good as it really is."

O.K. Maybe they've got a point. The VW is an amazingly advanced car.

The engine is a precision masterpiece, carved out of aluminum-magnesium alloy. It sits in back, over the drive wheels. The traction is unbelievable.

The engine is cooled by air. You simply never think about water or antifreeze.

Gas? Hardly any ever. Gas? About 26 miles per gallon of regular.

The Volkswagen's suspension is like a sports car's, its finish like a limousine's.

Almost anywhere you go in the world, VW has been before.

Its funny shape has become the international symbol of quality and reliability.

"Never change it," people beg us.

And now we beg the same of you.

Two ridiculous gimmicks of the 1940's.

Everyone laughed when they came out with the television.

A box that could show pictures from 3,000 miles away? Absurd.

But everyone really cracked up when we came out with the Volkswagen.

A car with its engine in the back? Its trunk in the front? And its radiator in neither the front nor the back?

It even looked like a joke.

But time marched on.

The television clicked.

The Volkswagen accelerated.

People liked the idea of a car that didn't drink gas like water. Or oil like water.

Or, for that matter, didn't even drink water.

Some strange people even liked the idea that it was strange looking.

In fact, Detroit car makers now like the idea of the VW so much that they have decided to make their own.

But even with all those new small cars around, the fate of the bug is still as secure as ever.

This is the first year for all of the others.

We've had twenty-three years of re-runs.

© VOLKSWAGEN OF AMERICA, INC.

"It was the only thing to do after the mule died."

Three years back, the Hinsleys of Dora, Missouri, had a tough decision to make.

To buy a new mule.

Or invest in a used bug.

They weighed the two possibilities.

First there was the problem of the bitter Ozark winters. Tough on a warm-blooded mule. Not so tough on an air-cooled VW.

Then, what about the eating habits of the two contenders? Hay vs. gasoline.

As Mr. Hinsley puts it: "I get over eighty miles out of a dollar's worth of gas and I get where I want to go a lot quicker."

Then there's the road leading to their cabin. Many a mule pulling a wagon and many a conventional automobile has spent many an hour stuck in the mud.

As for shelter, a mule needs a barn. A

bug doesn't. "It just sets out there all day and the paint job looks near as good as the day we got it."

Finally, there was maintenance to think about. When a mule breaks down, there's only one thing to do: Shoot it.

But if and when their bug breaks down, the Hinsleys have a Volkswagen dealer only two gallons away.

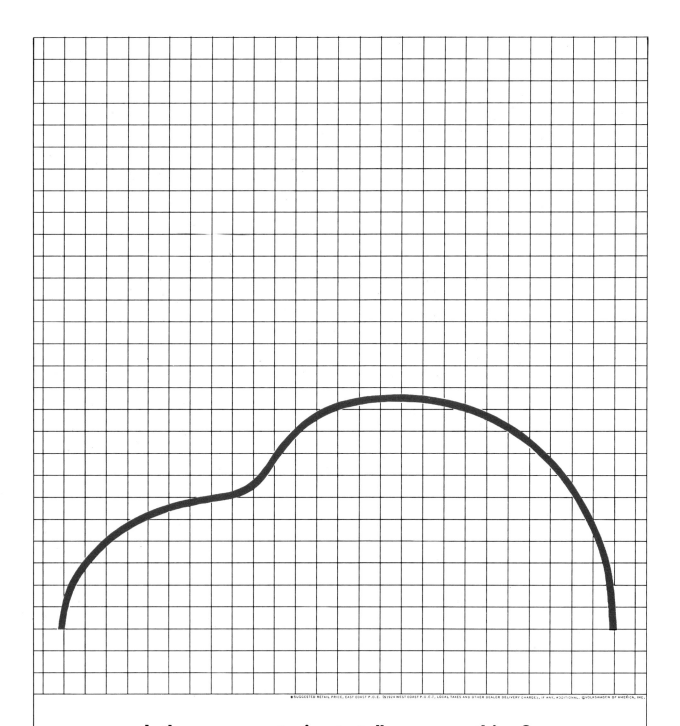

*SUGGESTED RETAIL PRICE, EAST COAST P.O.E. (§1924 WEST COAST P.O.E.), LOCAL TAXES AND OTHER DEALER DELIVERY CHARGES, IF ANY, ADDITIONAL. ©VOLKSWAGEN OF AMERICA, INC.

Is the economy trying to tell you something?

If you've hesitated about buying a new car because of the economy, maybe you should look into the economy of buying a new Volkswagen.

To begin with, while the average new car sells for about $3185, a new VW sells for only $1839*.

That saves you about $1300.

Then, while the average car costs 10.9 cents a mile to run, a Volkswagen costs only 5 cents.

That saves you about another $700 every year (or 12,000 miles) you drive.

And in just one year, it can bring your total savings to $2000.

In two years, $2700.

In three, $3400.

Happy days are here again.

1

Open on car showroom as an unsuspecting member of the public enters.

<u>Anncr:</u> He's here. Ladies and Gentlemen, the 18 millionth person in the world to buy a Volkswagen just walked through our doors.

<u>SFX:</u> Band strikes up.

2

<u>Anncr:</u> This is an historic moment. Excuse us boys. For who would have thought 22 years ago when only two Beetles were sold in the United States, that this day would come.

I'll tell you who. Volkswagen.

3

For a while everyone else was experimenting with new cars every year, Volkswagen stuck with one. Improving and refining it year after year. Until it has come to this, the 1971 Super Beetle. The 18 millionth Volkswagen made goes to. . . . Sorry, Sir, your name, Sir?

4

<u>Man:</u> Norman.

<u>Anncr:</u> Mr. Norman. What do you have to say about all this?

<u>Man:</u> Oh, I just wondered who ordered the tuna whole wheat, ice tea, no lemon. . .

<u>Anncr:</u> The what!

18 Millionth VW

*Suggested Retail Price Sedan 1111 P.O.E., local taxes and any other dealer delivery charges, if any, additional.
†Based on NADA Official Used Car Guide—April '74, (1972 P.O.E. vs. average used car retail prices).

Some of the most unusual things about a Volkswagen are things you don't usually see.

Look under the fender of a Volkswagen and you'll find something you couldn't dream of finding: paint.

We use 13 lbs. of it on every VW. And in the most unlikely places. (If you have nothing to do sometime, move one of our inside door panels and see what's underneath.)

Under the chassis of a Volkswagen you'll find something only a handful of cars in the world have: a sealed steel bottom. This protects all those vital things inside the car from all those vile things out there on the road. (Look under *your* car and you'll see how exposed and vulnerable everything is.)

See those four wheels sticking up in the air in the picture below? Well, you can press down on any one of them and move it without any of the others moving. What this means is when the car is right side up and one wheel hits a bump, none of the other wheels feel a thing.

Now, consider that you get all these luxury car features (and more) at an economy car price . . . with economy car gas mileage . . . the most advanced car coverage in the world (Owner's Security Blanket) . . . and almost unbelievable resale value (a '72 VW retails[†] for as much today as it did new).

You couldn't find a better buy if you stood on your head.

Still $2625[*]

©VOLKSWAGEN OF AMERICA, INC.

Presenting the 84 mpg Volkswagen.

Since all the car manufacturers are conducting their own mileage tests these days, we at Volkswagen thought we'd conduct one too.

So we modified our body—and our engine. And, of course, we got someone who didn't weigh much to drive.

Lo and behold, we got 84 miles per gallon! Ridiculous? Nobody normally drives like this? Of course. That's precisely our point.

Nobody normally drives like most of those tests you're seeing.

Volkswagen: An honest 25*miles per gallon.

105

When you're in trouble there's no place like home.

Sooner or later, your wife will drive home one of the best reasons for owning a Volkswagen.

After 3 years, the car that cost the least costs the most.

Take it for a test tan.

It takes this many men to

There are really only two things that stand between you and a new Volkswagen:

$1799.*

And 1,104 inspectors.

The money is your problem.

The number of inspectors it takes to okay each and every Volkswagen that leaves the Volkswagen factory is ours.

You see, once a man becomes a Full Inspector at our factory (and he'll spend three years doing just that), he becomes a different man.

He then has the power to overrule any and all decisions that relate to the manufacture of the car.

ect this many Volkswagens.

o'' from any one of those gentlemen up in the picture
olkswagen is not a Volkswagen.)

ngle VW part is inspected at least 3 times. That means
e the whole car can get from us to you, it has to go
,000 different inspections in all.
that: 16,000.

We lose an average of 225 Bugs a day that way.
So if you ever had to wait a little longer than you cared to
for a new Volkswagen, now you know why:
It's not that we can't make them fast enough.
It's just that we can't make them good enough
fast enough.

It's a bird. It's a plane. It's a Volkswagen?

That little plane up high in the sky is run by the same engine that runs our little car back down on the ground.

It belongs to Bob Ladd of Deer Park, N.Y.

And Bob belongs to a growing number of enthusiasts who happen to think there's only one way to fly. Via Volkswagen.

And why not?

A Volkswagen engine is dependable. (It's been dependable in over 10 million vehicles that never got off the ground.)

It's lightweight. (A nice feature to have at 10,000 feet.)

It's air-cooled. (No water or antifreeze to worry about.)

And most important of all, it doesn't drink much gas. (40 or 45 mpg seems to be what most flying VWs average.)

Safer Motoring Magazine calls a VW-powered aircraft from England "the most economical plane in the world today."

On one hand, we're really thrilled to hear that we're doing so well up high in the sky.

On the other, we don't recommend it. (In fact, we're against it.)

After all, if we had really meant the Volkswagen to fly, we would have made it look more like a bird. And less like a bug.

DOYLE DANE BERNBACH INC. ADVERTISING

NEW YORK, N. Y. 10036 LO 4-1234

RADIO · TELEVISION

program		air date	
client	VOLKSWAGEN	length	
product		job no.	

(sound: motorcycle pulling to a stop)

Policeman: Can I see your license?

Man: (laugh) Can you ever! Here you are! Hey, bet you didn't know a Volkswagen can move out like that, huh?

Policeman: Mmm. Take it out of your wallet please.

Man: Oh sure. What ya clock me at...'bout 80, 85?

Policeman: Can I see your registration?

Man: Oh yeah, here you go. Wait till I tell the guys at the plant, they said it couldn't be done...a ticket in a Volkswagen.

Policeman: Uh huh.

Man: Hey, you know officer, if you'd let me wind'er up I could have had it up to 95.

Policeman: This your present address?

Man: Yeah, uh huh, you know they increased the horsepower in these bugs... can't get over how they work.

Policeman: Uh huh.

Man: I wasn't even pushing it. hey, now really, how fast did you clock me? What are you writing down there?

Policeman: 65.

Man: 65!...are you kidding. Coming down that long hill I must have been doing 80, at least 75!

Policeman: Nope, 65.

Man : But 65 is the speed limit. What d'ya stop me for?

Policeman: That Bank job in Buffalo in '54.

Man: Oh.

Policeman: You want to get out that car?

Man: I bet I was doing 70.

Policeman: Slowly, get your hands behind your head.

Man: Couldn't you put 68?

© VOLKSWAGEN OF AMERICA, INC.

All good things must come to an end.

Volkswagens die. Like everything else. Only some people don't believe it.

Take Mrs. Carson Brooks of Oxford, Alabama. So far her '59 has gone over 600,000 miles. And that's with only two engine transplants.

Try telling her the end is near and she'll laugh you right off the farm.

That kind of owner loyalty begins at the VW factory where 100% of production time is spent making our little bug work better and 0% is spent making it look better (see ugly picture above).

It's the only car that's put through 15,397 inspections before it's put up for sale.

It won't give you radiator problems because we never gave it a radiator.

It comes fully equipped with 35 pounds of paint to protect its top and a protective steel bottom to protect its bottom.

So when you see one that looks on its last legs, feel no pity. It's probably led a healthier life than you have.

If gas pains persist, try Volkswagen.

©VOLKSWAGEN OF AMERICA, INC.

A VW goes a long way in relieving gas problems—by getting terrific gas mileage.

It also relieves those little headaches—by needing pints of oil instead of quarts. And <u>not</u> needing antifreeze.

Plus it gets rid of nervous upsets due to owning a new car. With Volkswagen's Owner's Security Blanket, you're provided with the best care any car can have…in sickness and in health.

The fact is Volkswagen can cure lots of problems that most cars can't.

Maybe you should take two.

The Volkswagen campaign had a profound effect on the US advertising industry.

Its simplicity and subtlety epitomised what good creative people fought for and bad clients fought against.

In 1963 the then young, but already influential magazine Communication Arts ran this tongue-in-cheek critique of the campaign. It was was featured again in a recent Anniversary issue. For good reason.

It all too accurately depicts the sort of small minded, heavy handed, belt and braces attitiude that still dogs the ad industry today, a full forty years later.

Nine Ways to Improve an Ad

BY FRED MANLEY

Back in 1963, Fred Manley, vice president and creative director of BBDO, San Francisco, made a tongue-in-cheek presentation to a local creative club on the subject of effective rules in advertising. Hal Riney created quick layout sketches for the art. Manley delivered it straight and it wasn't until the third or fourth "rule" that the audience began to see it as a farce. With Fred's permission, we ran it in our July/August 1963 issue with no explanation. The response was sensational, but we also got a few letters saying: "I don't agree with you" or "Didn't you guys make a mistake?" It's still our most requested article and it's still funny.

I'm sure you've seen a certain ad for the Volkswagen car, and heard it praised, and watched it pick up prizes the length and breadth of the land.

I'd like to nominate this ad as one of the most inept, most ineffectual, most misguided efforts of recent years.

Why? Because it's a perfect example of the disease that has spread throughout our business. A disease called "cleverness." Today, in some advertising quarters, cleverness is all that matters. You no longer have to have the selling idea. You no longer have to communicate that idea in clear, understandable terms. All you have to do is be witty. And amusing. And sophisticated. In short, "clever." And the more sane, sensible, tried-and-true rules you break along the way, the better.

The result, of course, is advertising like this. Advertising that titillates the precious few who work along Madison Avenue. That wins awards from ingrown groups of art directors. That makes conversation pieces at cocktail parties in Westport, Connecticut. Advertising that utterly fails to communicate with anyone who lives anywhere west of the Hudson River.

These are serious charges, I know—but I'm prepared to prove them. With your permission, I'd like to show you what this ad could have been—if only it hadn't worshipped at the shrine of cleverness. In short, with the sensitive aid of art director Hal Riney, I'd like to reconstruct it step-by-step, following the sensible rules that guide so much of advertising today.

Nine Ways to Improve an Ad

Rule: Show the product.

Don't turn it into a postage stamp or a test of failing eyesight. Show it. Boldly. Dramatically. Excitingly. Like this:

There. See the difference already? Now, I'll admit the headline no longer makes complete sense—but that brings us to another obvious improvement.

Rule: Don't use negative headlines.

"Think Small" may be very clever, very witty....but what an idea to leave in the minds of everyday readers.

"Think BIG!" Now I ask you—isn't that better? Isn't it more positive, more direct? And note, too, the interesting use of type to punch home the excitement of the idea.

Well that brings us to still another improvement—and one of the most important rules in advertising.

Rule: Whenever possible, mention your product name in the headline.

Which the people who thought up this ad could have done so very, very easily.

See how the ad is beginning to jell? How it's really starting to come alive.

Let's see another way we can breathe some life into it—with a warming touch of humanity.

Rule: Whenever possible, show people enjoying your product.

That's more like it. A gracious mansion. A carefree band of dancers. And best of all, a proud pair of thoroughbreds.

Now for an improvement to correct a fault in the product itself. You'll note that the VW, unfortunately, is totally lacking in news. From year to year, while other cars bring out a host of exciting changes—it stays its own dowdy self.

Rule: Always feature news in your advertisement. And if you have no news, invent it. Like this:

How's that for news?

Rule: (One of the most obvious of the bunch) **Always give prominent display to your product logo.**

And I don't mean an arty jumble of initials no one can read; I mean a proud unashamed logo like this:

There. Now they know who's paying for the ad!

Rule: Avoid all unpleasant connotation about your product.

Which brings us to a somewhat delicate area: the country of origin of the Volkswagen car. Now I don't have to dwell on the subject of World War II and its attendant unpleasantness for you to grasp my meaning. Let's simply say that it might be wise to "domesticate" the car, so to speak.

VOLKSWAGEN—THE ALL–AMERICAN CAR!

And in a flash, apple strudel turns into good old apple pie!

Rule: Always tell the reader where he can buy your product.

Where can you buy a Volkswagen?

"At your friendly authorized Volkswagen dealer." Note the warmth of words like "friendly." And the use of "Authorized" to make sure that prospects don't stumble into places that are unauthorized.

One rule to go. The most important rule of all.

Rule: Always localize your ads.

And mind the way you spell the dealer's names.

There you have it. No clever, precious, self-conscious waste of space like the ad we started with; but an honest hard-hitting, two-fisted ad like this that really sells.

I said "sells." ■

The Station Wagon.

Volkswagen's vans and trucks did very well in the early sixties, selling over 30,000 a year to butchers, bakers, candlestick makers and the like.

But in 1961 sales were brought to a standstill by the "Chicken War", an import duty tit-for-tat that raised the price of US poultry reaching Germany and German light trucks reaching the USA.

The new high rates of duty did not apply to passenger versions of the VW van, but initially it seemed unlikely that these would ever sell in sufficient numbers to compensate for the sizeable lost truck volume.

American women in particular disliked the vehicle and in the early sixties the market for campers was very small indeed.

Think tall.

Our Volkswagen Station Wagon is only nine inches longer than our little VW Sedan. Yet it holds more than the biggest conventional wagon.

How?

Perhaps this picture explains it.

Ideally in a station wagon, you need maximum room and minimum length. We have answered this with a taller car. (The entire top of the VW wagon is level. This gives it the shape of a box. There is not a wasted inch in it.)

This is why things that will not fit in any conventional wagon fit easily inside the VW wagon.

An upright piano standing upright. A standard bridge table opened up. Eight adults with all their luggage.

Or, if you open the sun-roof, a huge old-fashioned wooden wardrobe. Even a horse fifteen hands high.

People are pleased that our VW wagon parks so easily. (If you have ever circled a shopping mart or a commuters' station looking for a big enough space for your big wagon, you can appreciate this.)

 When you realize our VW Station Wagon is a good four feet shorter than conventional wagons, you get the picture.

It carries a boatload.

That's a Volkswagen Station Wagon, all dressed up in ship's clothing.

. Inside, it's big enough to swallow up a whole sailboat. Yet you can park it in about the same space as a VW Sedan.

When it isn't carrying boats, the wagon takes on 8 people, luggage and all.

Or practically a ton of anything else.

Just to give you an idea, it can handle a piano (with player) or an open bridge table (with 4 players).

There's a gaping 4-foot door on the side to load things into, and a sunroof on top to stick things out of.

There's also some sweet satisfaction in having a wagon that's so cheap to run.

You can expect 24 miles to the gallon, for example. 35,000 miles on a set of tires. And an air-cooled engine that never needs water or antifreeze.

If you already own a VW Station Wagon, don't let people kid you about its shape.

. Just carry on.

When you stop at a gas station, it's usually not to get gas.

And it's not to get oil.

And it's not to get water. (The Volkswagen engine is air-cooled.)

And it's not to stretch your legs, because the Volkswagen Station Wagon seats 9 with comfort—and with luggage—though it's 4 feet shorter than a conventional wagon.

If the world looked like this,
and you wanted to buy a car that sticks out a little,
you probably wouldn't buy a Volkswagen Station Wagon.
   But in case you haven't noticed, the world doesn't look like this.
   So if you've wanted to buy a car that sticks out a little,
you know just what to do.

This station wagon seats 8. Sometimes.

This is our two-faced Volkswagen. When it's not acting like a station wagon, it works like a horse.

All you do is take out the seats. And you do this by turning six wing nuts. This leaves you with a great emptiness. Which you can fill with 1,786 lbs. of anything you like.

This model is called the Kombi. It's the same size as our deluxe wagon. And has the same VW traction in snow and sand. The legendary VW gas mileage. An air-cooled engine that can never freeze up or boil over. Etc.

But it's only $2,195.

It's not only low for a station wagon, it's even low for a Volkswagen station wagon!

But then you may not want to use it as a station wagon at all. That's your business.

How does it feel to show up in one of these?

Odd.

But nobody expects you to jump right into the social whirl with a Volkswagen Station Wagon.

It's even O.K. to be a coward at first.

Buy it on a Tuesday and take a long trip with the family on Wednesday.

Don't worry about summer or winter, the VW's air-cooled engine can't freeze up or boil over.

Don't worry a bit about the size of your family, either. The VW carries more than even the biggest anonymous wagons.

When you're back home, the whole trick is to drive it a little later every day.

Once you're sure of yourself at the A&P and the lumberyard, venture out at night. Try an early movie. Then a late dinner.

Then shoot the works.

You're free to invent your own method, of course, but this one usually works.

The thing we don't understand is why people feel better about driving a VW Station Wagon in broad daylight than they do at night.

You'd think it would be the other way around.

170 cubic feet of station wagon.

This picture may look a little odd. But so are most conventional station wagons when you consider how little they hold.

The two above only average about 85 cubic feet each.

The Volkswagen Station Wagon holds twice that: 170.

And even if you did put two conventional wagons together you still couldn't carry the kind of things you can in a Volkswagen.

It has a 14-square-foot hole in the roof for sticking tall things out of.

And five big doors for sticking things into.

On the inside, the VW has seats for 9 people and room for 28 cubic

170 cubic feet of station wagon.

feet of luggage.
(Not "or" 28 cubic feet.)

But on the outside, it's only 9 inches longer than the VW Sedan. You can park it like a sports car.

And everywhere you go, the

VW engine is right behind you.

It goes over 20 miles on a gallon of regular gas. And you never have to pay for antifreeze, flushings, or radiator repair.

There isn't any radiator.

And you can safely expect 15,000 extra miles on your tires. (Ours average 35,000 miles.)

When you think about it, the VW Station Wagon not only holds a pile, it can also save you one.

Got a lot to carry? Get a box.

Now add a few seats. Say 8.

Make an aisle so you can walk to the back.

Cut a hole in the roof to let the sun in.

Windows? At least 21. Doors? 5 should do.

Paint it up and what have you got?

The whole idea behind the Volkswagen Station Wagon.

© VOLKSWAGEN OF AMERICA, INC

The Volkswagen is the big one.

We know our wagon is five feet shorter than the other model.

But we still say it's bigger because it holds more: 170 cubic feet.

(Regular wagons vary from 57 to 91.)

To understand how we get the extra room, you have to appreciate the shape of the Volkswagen Station Wagon.

It's built like a big box — taller than it is wide.

(A good-sized kid can walk down the aisle standing up.)

There is virtually no wasted space on the VW. Even the engine is tucked away. (Over the drive wheels.)

You can carry 8 big adults with luggage.

Or 1632 lbs. of assorted children.

And if you slide the sunroof back you can lug home a big day at the auction.

Big as our wagon is, it's only 9 inches longer than the Volkswagen Sedan.

So if you're ever in a tight jam, it can seem pretty small.

Why won't your wife let you buy this wagon?

"It looks like a bus."

"I wouldn't be caught dead in it."

Do these sound familiar? Your wife is not alone. It is hard to convince some women what sense the VW Station Wagon makes.

Its chunky shape, for instance, allows it to hold more than the biggest conventional wagon. (Yet it is a good four feet shorter, and a lot less exasperating to park.)

She might like the easy way it loads. The side doors give her almost 16 sq. ft. for big supermarket bags, a baby carriage, etc.

The Volkswagen Station Wagon does not have to take anything lying down. She can cart home an antique chest, standing up. Or delicate trees from the nursery. (Wide things, too. It will hold an open playpen.)

She can comfortably pack in eight or more Scouts, with all their cook-out gear.

She can give the family some extra sun on the way to the beach. (Why no other station wagon has a sun-roof is a mystery.)

Even if the traffic is bumper to bumper on hot days, she will not have to worry about the radiator boiling over. There is no radiator, no water. (The Volkswagen engine is air cooled.)

She may get a kick out of beeping to the other women who drive VW Station Wagons. (They have a kind of private club.)

Or maybe she likes to see where she is going. (The VW wagon has incredible visibility on hills and curves.)

If these facts don't convince her, why not give up gracefully.

(For this year, anyway.)

Be the first on your block.

Most cars are as uncontroversial as mashed potatoes.

Not the Volkswagen Station Wagon. People either love it or hate it.

How do you feel about its boxy body? Its flat roof? Its bus-like shape?

Do you know these allow it to carry more than the biggest conventional station wagon? And still be 4 feet shorter? And

miles easier to park?

Does it seem odd that the VW is the only wagon with 23 windows and a sun-roof?

Do you know what a tremendous view this gives you? That you see more sky and skyline than in any other car, except a convertible with the top down?

Why can you order a VW wagon with

seats that include an aisle?

Do you know that this lets you walk back to the kids from the front seat? In case they cry or quarrel or get the million ills that kids are heir to?

Does the VW Station Wagon seem so strange to you now?

Or does it make a busload of sense?

That's a load off our front.

Now you know why the Volkswagen Station Wagon has that sawed-off look.

There is no front in front because we put our engine in back.

The advantages are obvious.

The Volkswagen is 4 feet shorter than standard wagons, but only 9 inches longer than the Volkswagen Sedan.

It parks like a little sports car.

Yet inside, you can carry more stuff than any wagon made: 1632 lbs.

Then there are a couple of advantages that aren't so obvious.

The VW is nearly a ton lighter on its tires than standard wagons. So 35,000 miles to a set is not unusual.

And you'll never need water. Or anti-freeze. The engine's air-cooled.

You get the kind of mileage people hope for in compact cars, to say nothing of big wagons. (24 mpg is average.)

And you're still pushing a hood in front? When all that could be behind you?

Box yourself in.

The Volkswagen Station Wagon looks like a box because it's built like a box.

It lets you store the most possible stuff in the least possible space.

(The fact is, the VW carries more than the biggest regular wagons, even though it's 4 feet shorter.)

The VW's floor plan looks like any nice little room, except that it has 8 chairs, 21 windows, 5 doors and a high ceiling.

You can't see the engine because it's in the back, out of the way.

If you aren't the curious type, you may never see the engine. No reason to. It rarely uses oil between changes. And it's air-cooled, so there's no water or antifreeze.

But the real fun comes when you climb into the box and get behind the wheel.

Ahead of you, there's nothing but view; it's head and shoulders above other cars.

Behind you, there's nothing but space.

It looks a mile long, but it's really only 9 inches longer than the Volkswagen Sedan.

So you can park it like the Sedan.

And like the Sedan, you get a lot of extras (heater/defroster, electric clock, etc.) at no extra cost.

We've put everything we could think of into it.

So will you.

We also make a funny-looking car.

We make a car that looks like a beetle. And a station wagon that looks like a bus. (Or so we're told.)

But we think of them a little differently; both Volkswagens look just like what they are.

The VW Sedan is for carrying 4 people. The station wagon is for carrying 8, bag and baggage. (With almost as much headroom

and legroom as you get in a real bus.)

The wagon also handles a staggering amount of just stuff. (It has 170 cubic feet of space, compared to about 105 in conventional wagons.)

Both Volkswagens have air-cooled rear engines. No water or anti-freeze needed; terrific traction on ice and snow.

Both park in practically the same space. (The wagon is only 9 inches longer.)

Both defy obsolescence. Nobody knows what year VW you drive. Except you.

Our sedan is a pretty familiar sight; not many people laugh at it any more. But our station wagon is still good for a few chuckles.

That's about the size of it.

That special paint job is to make it perfectly clear that our Station Wagon is only 9 inches longer than our Sedan.

Yet it carries almost a ton of anything you like. (About twice as much as you can get into wagons that are 4 feet longer.)

Or eight solid citizens, with luggage.

Or countless kids, with kid stuff.

The things you never think about are worth thinking about, too.

You never worry about freezing or boiling; the rear engine is air-cooled.

You can expect about 24 miles per gallon and about 30,000 miles on your tires.

And you can forget about going out of style next year; next year's model will look the same.

The most expensive VW Station Wagon costs $2,655.* It comes in red and white or grey and white or green and white.

And you won't ever have to go around painting sedans on it to show how small it is.

Just park.

What is it?

Glad you asked.

It's a Volkswagen Station Wagon.

Don't pity the poor thing; it can take it.

It can carry nearly a ton of anything you can afford to buy.

Or 8 people (plus luggage) if you want to get practical about it.

And there's more than one practical consideration.

It will take you about 24 miles on a gallon of regular gas.

It won't take any water or anti-freeze at all; the engine is air-cooled.

And even though it carries almost twice as much as regular wagons, it takes 4 feet less to park.

What's in the package?

8 pairs of skis, the complete works of Dickens, 98 lbs. of frozen spinach, a hutch used by Grover Cleveland, 80 Hollywood High gym sweaters, a suit of armor, and a full sized reproduction of the Winged Victory of Samothrace.

Doyle Dane Bernbach Inc.

1

Open on angry mob attacking
mysterious castle.

2

MVO: If you've created a
rather large family, and you
have an awful lot to carry.

3

And you want to get away from
it all - chances are your
normal station wagon won't
be large enough.

4

So maybe you ought to consider
something not quite so normal.

Like the Volkswagen.

Castle

Somebody actually stole one.

We were tickled pink to hear that somebody wanted a Volkswagen Station Wagon badly enough to go out and steal one.

It wasn't so long ago that we practically couldn't give them away.

So when Martin Carlson reported his loss to the police, we took it as a triumph.

In its own way, the VW Station Wagon is one of the world's best getaway cars.

You can escape north or south of the border. (The VW engine can't freeze up or boil over because it's cooled by air.)

You can go farther in a VW than in any police car (24 mpg is our average).

You have 21 windows to spot anyone who's tailing you.

And it carries more loot (170 cu. ft.) than the biggest regular wagon you can steal.

Sadly, the whole theory blew apart when Mr. Carlson found his VW abandoned in the very spot he had left it.

Maybe everyone isn't ready for it, after all.

Not even crooks.

You'll never lose it in a parking lot.

You can see where a Volkswagen Station Wagon comes in handy.

You don't have to tie a handkerchief to the aerial to find your way back.

But we didn't make it stick up just to make it stand out.

We made it that way simply because it made sense.

When you make a wagon that tall, it will hold more. Almost twice as much, in fact, as conventional wagons.

And when you put the engine in the rear, you can lop off the hood and have four feet less wagon to park.

There's also less gas to buy. (You should average about 24 miles per gallon.)

And absolutely no antifreeze. Our engine is air-cooled.

But what's really nice is that something so flagrantly practical is such fun to drive.

Even on a routine trip to the supermarket.

O. K. So you stick out a little. Maybe it's time?

Ever wonder who buys them?

We did, too.

So we hired a very expensive research company to find people who own Volkswagen Station Wagons and ask them.

On some topics, we could have saved the money.

People with 2.4 children

It came as no shock to find that an overwhelming number of people bought VW Station Wagons because they wanted a wagon that carried a lot and that was cheap to run.

But it was a surprise to learn that people really aren't taking advantage of the VW Station Wagon's size.

The VW holds twice what regular wagons hold: over a ton. (The VW can hold 10 kids with no trouble at all.)

Yet the average family that buys one has only 2.4 children. (Maybe they all have big plans and aren't talking.)

Sometimes, all the extra space turns into a problem. "Once in a while I have to borrow somebody else's wagon," a man complained. "Because everybody else keeps borrowing mine."

Roughly half the VW owners have no other car, so the VW Station Wagon gets used for all their driving.

The other half own more than one car, but 94% use the VW for most of their driving anyway.

"It's more fun," is the usual reason.

We were fascinated to find that some people (9%) own a great big conventional station wagon in addition to the VW. "I use the big one when I don't have too much to carry," a lady muttered.

There is also an astonishing number (14%) who drive both a Volkswagen Station Wagon and a Volkswagen Sedan.

"Why?" we asked.

"Why not?" we were answered.

48% are 2 or more car people

52% are 1 car people

The average income of our owners is a little under $175 a week.

But we get all kinds. About 1% of the owners earn less than $3,000 a year. And another 1% earn over $50,000.

So the VW is very democratic. The rich man saves as much money on gas, oil, tires and antifreeze as the poor man.

Volkswagen Station Wagon owners are pretty well educated: 6 out of 10 went to college and 4 out of 10 were

6 out of 10 are college people

graduated. (Which doesn't prove much, except that you don't have to be absolutely crazy to buy one.)

We seem to have a high number of doctors, lawyers, teachers, foremen, etc.

And they seem to be quite young: half the owners are under 35.

Something that pleased us is that 57% bought the VW Station Wagon because we have a reputation for making a good product. (40%, in fact, didn't even consider buying anything else.)

On the other hand, it displeased us that not even 1% bought it because they thought it had good traction in mud and snow. (Evidently, nobody pays much attention to what we say in our ads.)

All in all, we were happy to learn that VW Station Wagon owners are such nice, sober, industrious citizens.

They think of their wagons (and themselves) as something special.

And they keep them for a long time because they hold up and stay in style.

(A VW Station Wagon always looks exactly as preposterous as the day you drove it home.)

100% of the people who own Volkswagen Station Wagons couldn't care less.

If you can sell her on this, you can sell her on anything.

"Me? In *that*?"

When you take your wife to see the Volkswagen Station Wagon don't be surprised if you have to drag her.

"But it looks silly."

That's your first problem: you have to explain the flat face and square shape.

The front is flat because the engine is in the back. This eliminates a long hood and makes our wagon almost as easy to park as our sedan. (There's only 9 inches difference.)

And the square shape holds almost twice as much as an everyday station wagon: 170 cubic feet.

Once you coax her behind the wheel, be ready for something like this:

"But it's like sitting in a fishbowl." She's right, it is. There are 21 windows all around.

And if she handles the family checkbook, you might show her a few numbers:

24 mpg on regular. 35,000 miles on tires. 4 pints of oil, not 4 quarts.

If you can sell your wife on the VW Station Wagon, consider yourself a star salesman.

We certainly will.

Doyle Dane Bernbach Inc.

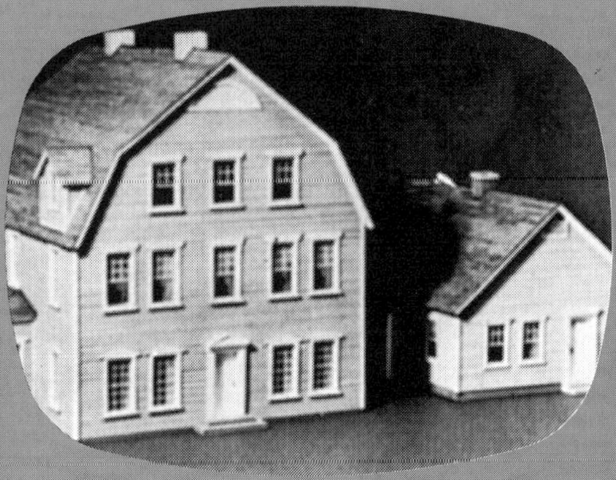

1

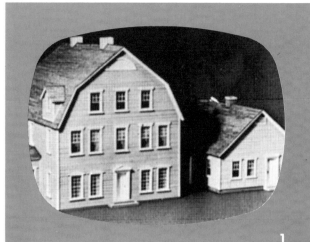

Open on slide show.

Signor W: Okay Johnny, are you ready for your lesson?

Johnny: I am ready.

Signor W: Good. First slide please. Now, Johnny. The big house holds more people than the little house. Which one costs more?

Johnny: The big house.

Signor W: Very good. Next please.

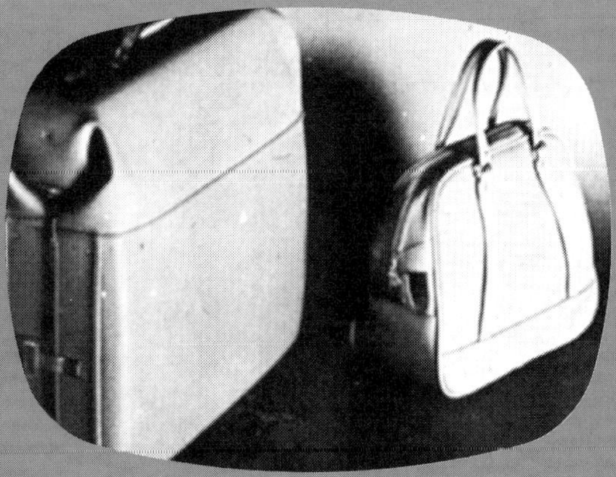

2

Signor W: Now Johnny, the big suitcase holds more things than the little suitcase. Which one costs more?

Johnny: The big suitcase.

Signor W: Very good. Next please.

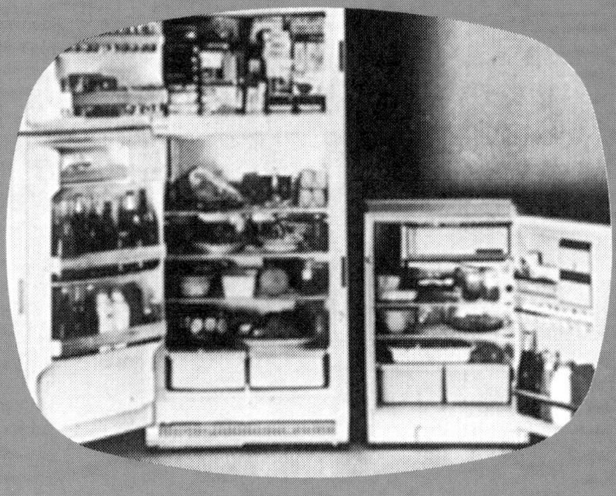

3

Signor W: Now Johnny, the big refrigerator has more cubic feet than the little refrigerator. Which one costs more?

Johnny: The big refrigerator.

Signor W: Very good.

Johnny: Very easy

Signor W: Next slide, please.

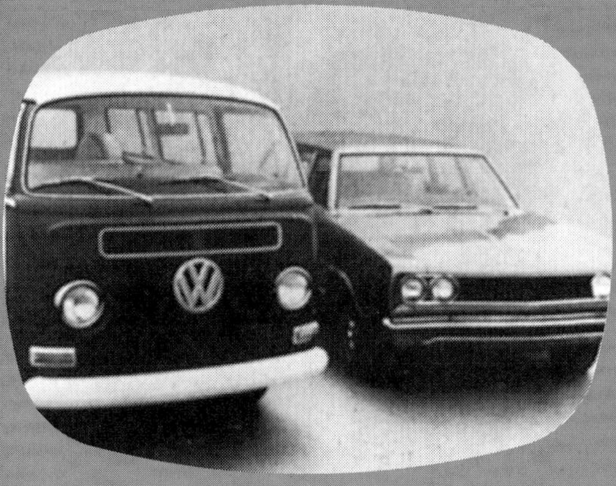

4

Signor W: OK Johnny, the big Volkswagen stationwagon holds more people,carries more things and has twice as much cubic feet than the little stationwagon.Now,which one costs more?

Johnny: The big Volkswagen.

Signor W: No, Johnny, the big Volkswagen costs much less.

Johnny: I don't understand.

Signor W I don't understand either.
Man in Box: It's alright.

Senor Wences

A beautiful day to own a Volkswagen Station Wagon.

On Monday, January 24, 1966, an estimated 262,825,033.74 tons of snow fell upon the United States of America.

In Fraser, Colorado, a VW Station Wagon that stood for days out in temperatures of 25 below, started up without a tremble.

In Scarsdale, a lonely VW was blazing a trail to the commuter station.

In Albany, a VW took 8 angry neighbors down to the local service station for 8 sets of chains.

In Moline, a VW woman was first in line at the A&P Steak Sale.

Up in Boston, a group of college kids were finding out how many toboggans they could stuff into 170 cubic feet of VW space.

A Milwaukee junior hockey team won its game by default.

On Monday, January 24, 1966, not too many Volkswagens were sold in the United States.

On Tuesday, things picked up.

Progress.

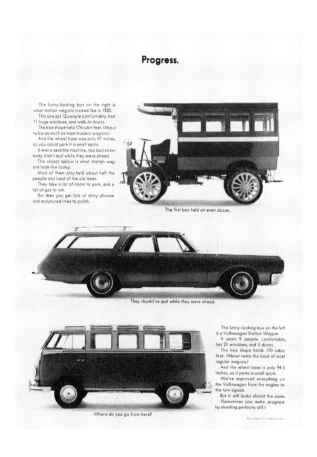

The funny-looking box on the right is what station wagons looked like in 1920.

This one sat 12 people comfortably, had 11 huge windows, and walk-in doors.

The box shape held 174 cubic feet. (About twice as much as most modern wagons.)

And the wheel base was only 97 inches, so you could park it in small spots.

It was a sensible machine; too bad somebody didn't quit while they were ahead.

The object below is what station wagons look like today.

Most of them only hold about half the people and load of the old timer.

They take a lot of room to park, and a lot of gas to run.

But then you get lots of shiny chrome and sculptured lines to polish.

The first box held an even dozen.

They should've quit while they were ahead.

The funny-looking box on the left is a Volkswagen Station Wagon.

It seats 9 people comfortably, has 21 windows, and 5 doors.

The box shape holds 170 cubic feet. (About twice the load of most regular wagons.)

And the wheel base is only 94.5 inches, so it parks in small spots.

We've improved everything on the Volkswagen from the engine to the turn signals.

But it still looks almost the same. (Sometimes you make progress by standing perfectly still.)

Where do you go from here?

We learned something from the big boys.

We're not above borrowing a good idea when we see one.

And the idea of a station wagon with all the virtues of a bus was too good to resist.

Which is why the VW Station Wagon has so much in common with other buses.

The driver is way up front, so he can see where he's going.

The engine is in back, out of the way.

There are windows all around (21 in all) including the skylight kind on top.

The seats are chair-high. And you can even have an aisle to step to the rear.

The Volkswagen Station Wagon has a bit less headroom than a real bus, but it has more doors (5) and a sunroof that slides back for lots of air and lots of view.

There's so much room inside the VW,

you may think you're driving the real thing.

But not when you park; the VW Wagon is only 9 inches longer than the VW Sedan.

Lately, we've spotted a few other bus-type station wagons on the scene.

So maybe things have worked out evenly after all.

The big boys learned something from us.

The engine's in the back.

Tell the truth.

Did you know right off that it was just a Volkswagen Campmobile? Or did you think it was really a place to live?

It's an easy mistake to make because the VW Campmobile is really more like a house than a car.

There are curtains and screens on the windows, wood paneling on the insulated walls, and wall-to-wall covering on the floor. (All standard equipment.)

Two adults and two kids can sleep in it, eat in it, wash in it

and keep their clothes and food in it.

And if the old scenery gets dreary, just fold the optional tent and move on.

Of course, it isn't a house. It's a Volkswagen. With all the things that make a Volkswagen a Volkswagen.

But no matter what we say, lots of people go on making the same mistake.

We keep saying it's a Campmobile.

And they keep saying it's a place to live.

They laughed.

3000 B.C. Somebody invented the wheel. It was round and funny. And since the road wasn't invented yet, everybody laughed.

1879. The electric light bulb. It was so dim, people had to use a gas lamp to see it. They laughed.

1875. The telephone. Who'd want to stand and talk to a box full of wires? They laughed.

1877. The automobile sputtered down the road. The horse and buggy passed it like it was standing still. And it usually was.

1807. The first steamboat in America made it from New York to Albany in 32 hours. A small boy could've beat it in a rowboat. They laughed.

1903. The airplane. Off it soared into the wild blue yonder. down it came 59 seconds later. They laughed.

1950. The Volkswagen Station Wagon. It was square and homely. But it held almost twice as much as un-funny wagons, took 4 feet less space to park, never froze up or boiled over, and cost about half as much to run.

The VW Wagon is still a pretty funny sight. And people are still laughing. But the laughter is dying down.

Should you pay twice as much to get it washed?

A Volkswagen isn't any bigger than other station wagons . . . it just carries more.

That's because a station wagon shaped like a box can hold about twice as much as a station wagon shaped like a station wagon.

So it will cost you exactly the same to get it washed, but that's about all that will cost you exactly the same.

Our VW Wagon gets around 23 miles to the gallon.

You'll pay Volkswagen prices for parts. Some 35,000 miles should go by before you have to go buy new tires.

And come to think of it, maybe you should pay less for the wash job, too.

A Volkswagen is actually shorter than other station wagons. (It'll park in 4' less space.)

So next time, why not ask the man at the car wash for a discount.

Don't tell him we sent you.

You never know when you'll hav

That's a Volkswagen Station Wagon with an elephant almost in it.

The part that doesn't quite fit in can stick out, because our VW wagon has a sunroof. And the part that does fit, fits because a VW has 170 cu. ft. of space.

(Most ordinary wagons offer only 90 or 100 cu. ft. of space. Also, they don't have a 4' wide door in their side for 4' wide things to get through.)

The fact is, a VW can carry almost twice as much as an ordinary wagon. But an ordinary wagon can't always

take an elephant someplace.

carry half as much as a VW. Because some things are hard to split up.

Like an elephant, for instance, or a breakfront, or a rolltop desk, or a combo practicing on the way to a job.

So just because you managed to get through today without one of our wagons, doesn't mean that something big won't come up tomorrow.

The truth is, nobody really needs a Volkswagen Station Wagon . . . until they really need one.

Doyle Dane Bernbach Inc.

1

Open on camper pulling up in misty 'horror movie' landscape.

2

<u>Sinister MVO</u>: There is a legend that they tell, that when the sun goes down and the moon comes up.

3

There is a car that turns into a house.

4

<u>SFX</u>: Wolf howling.

Bela Lugosi

It comes in its own box.

There has to be a little Scrooge in you to give a Volkswagen Station Wagon for Christmas.

Because when you open it up, it's just a big, empty box.

It has nearly twice the room as conventional wagons that don't look like boxes.

It holds 9 conventional adults or who-knows-how-many unconventional kids.

Or you can put a 40-foot Christmas tree right through the hole in the roof.

You can carry 170 cubic feet of snow or go skiing with the skis inside.

At this time of year, you'll enjoy the VW's firm traction. (The engine is in back, over the drive wheels.)

And you'll never spend a dime on anti-freeze; the engine is air-cooled. (Which also means it can't boil over next summer.)

There are a few other tight-fisted items you'll go for: 35,000 miles on a set of tires, over 20 mpg and hardly any oil between changes.

Let us hear from you, Scrooge.

The Volkswagen Station Wagon holds

Jiggs, Nevada is populated by five adults, four children, and one big dog that doesn't like photographers.

That happens to be just how many you can comfortably seat in a Volkswagen Station Wagon.

(In fact, the VW not only holds the whole town of Jiggs, it also holds about twice as much as a conventional wagon: 170 cubic feet.)

Next to people, the scarcest thing in Jiggs is gasoline. There's only one pump

in the whole town. You have to drive 2. miles to get to the next one.

And you could get to the next one in VW on about one gallon of gas.

O. A. Breschini, who runs the only sa loon in Jiggs ("We haven't had a shootin

OK here:

e entire population of Jiggs, Nevada.

wo years.") says the summers get better n 105° above.

And Will Peters, who makes the best ote bait in Elko County, remembers the ter of '36 when it got near 50° below. ortunately, there's nothing in the VW that can freeze or boil. The engine's air-cooled, so it gets along just beautifully.

Once we got all the people in, they liked the seats, windows and sunroof so much we didn't know how to ask them to get out.

So we contributed one brand-new Volkswagen Station Wagon to the town of Jiggs, Nevada and rode off into the fading sunset.

(Sometimes it pays a town not to get too big.)

Old Volkswagen Station Wagons never die.

The things some people can do with an old box.

But then, he didn't start with any old box.

He started with a Volkswagen Station Wagon. Which has about twice the amount of space as an ordinary wagon.

There was room for everything.

A refrigerator, a stove, a table, an instant chili dispenser, and of course, the proverbial kitchen sink.

And a way for it all to get in. The two side doors open into a huge 4' by 4' hole.

Also, its roof may be high compared to other wagons, but its overhead is low. Our Standard VW wagon costs only $2,337.*

However, if you're planning to go into the restaurant business, better not buy one new. (The body's been welded into one solid piece of steel, the tires alone will last for 35,000 miles, and on top of everything else, there are four coats of protective paint.)

It'll take too long to get a new one into bad enough shape.

A Volkswagen station wagon will now go 5,000 miles on a dime.

The people of the Republic of Dahomey have given us their stamp of approval.

After years of traipsing over unpaved jungle roads carrying 176 cubic feet of palm oil and coffee beans in the hot African sun without the benefit of water and without the need for lots of gasoline, the Volkswagen Station Wagon has become a national hero.

So the good people of the Republic of Dahomey have put its picture on their national stamp.

Once again it was simply a case of our economy helping someone else's economy.

Can it really carry as much as we say?

Ask the man who borrows one.

The man on the right owns a conventional station wagon.

It's got twice the style of a Volkswagen Station Wagon, but only about half the carrying space.

So when he has more to carry than his wagon can handle in one trip, a trip next door can save him a trip.

Or, if he has something extra big to bring home, like an upright piano, he can bring it home in his neighbor's Volkswagen. Upright.

(Our wagon has an unusually high roof, and an unusually wide 4' door in its side.)

But then maybe you don't live next door to a Volkswagen Station Wagon. In that case, you might want to buy one.

The Deluxe Model has 21 windows and a sliding sunroof. It seats 9 comfortably. It gets around 23 miles to the gallon. Its tires will last for about 35,000 miles. And it parks in 4' less space than most conventional wagons.

Of course, if for some reason you can't buy one, there's always the next best thing... talk your neighbor into buying one.

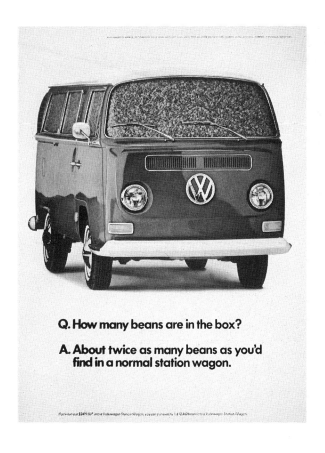

Q. How many beans are in the box?

A. About twice as many beans as you'd find in a normal station wagon.

Open wide and say ah.

Surprise.
You thought you were going to see a roomy, homely Volkswagen station wagon.
But it's a new kind of roomy, homely Volkswagen station wagon.
To begin with, getting in is easier: the front doors are lower and wider. And with the side door we've achieved a milestone in station wagon doordom. It slides.

Once inside, you might even think you're in a normal car. Everything's padded. Including the dashboard, visors, and the armrests. (Besides looking like a car, we've improved the suspension so it even rides like a car.)
There are bucket seats up front. And where most cars have something called a console, the new box has an aisle. (If the

mood should strike you, you can walk the length of the box.)
So when you look inside the new box expect to be pleasantly surprised. But not overwhelmed.
Because as boxes go, our station wagon is now pretty fancy.
But as station wagons go, it's still a box.

It carries as much as the average station wagon.

Believe it or not, this half of a VW Station Wagon wouldn't be a bad thing to own.
Because half a Volkswagen Station Wagon holds as much as most whole wagons hold.
Half a VW Station Wagon gives you a gaping 88 cubic feet of carrying space.
It can haul a whole 1185 pounds of one thing and another.
It can carry a whatchamacallit 4 ft. tall.
It transports 4.5 solid citizens, 6.5 big pieces of luggage and none of the latter has to sit with the former.
Even half a VW Station Wagon still gets up to 23 miles to the gallon, and doesn't use any water or antifreeze.
But best of all, half a Volkswagen Station Wagon would cost you only $1301.
And that's only half the story.

It carries as much as the average station wagon.

Believe it or not, this half of a VW Station Wagon wouldn't be a bad thing to own.
Because half a Volkswagen Station Wagon holds as much as most whole wagons hold.
Half a VW Station Wagon gives you a gaping 88 cubic feet of carrying space.
It can haul a whole 1185 pounds of one thing and another.
It can carry a whatchamacallit 4 ft. tall.
It transports 4.5 solid citizens, 6.5 big pieces of luggage and none of the latter has to sit with the former.
Even half a VW Station Wagon still gets up to 23 miles to the gallon, and doesn't use any water or antifreeze.
But best of all, half a Volkswagen Station Wagon would cost you only $1301.
And that's the whole story.

Escape thy neighbor.

And find some peace with a little help from a friend, the Volkswagen Campmobile.

If you be weary, you shall be comforted by soft beds, airy curtains, wood paneled walls, and plenty of room to breathe.

For those who hunger and thirst, there's an icebox, a kitchen table, and plenty of cool drinking water.

And for those who fear that the path to that special place will be hard to follow, worry not. Thanks be to our powerful rear mounted engine and new fully automatic transmission, you can go where you like.

The sky's the limit.

The house that Volkswagen built.

It may be no glittering mansion. But it can provide what any good house can provide.

If you want rest, you'll find rest. It has enough sleeping accommodations for a family of 5.

If you want to wash up, you can wash up. It has a sink and a 4½ gallon supply of water.

If you want to eat, eat. It has a pantry, a dining room table and a 2.7 cu. ft. icebox.

It has a closet for linen. A closet for clothes. And no less than 3 large storage cabinets for all your other stuff.

Compared to the other houses built, the house that Volkswagen built costs very little. $3,382.*

Of course, there's one trait that really sets it apart.

If you become unhappy with the place you're in, VW Campmobile can do something no other house ever built can do.

It can move you to greener pastures at about 23 miles on a gallon of gas.

In 5 minutes it had better turn into a station wagon.

When something tells you to break camp fast, the Volkswagen Campmobile is an easy camp to break.

The tent folds up in four minutes and the roof clamps shut in 10 seconds. Which leaves you 50 seconds to tidy up inside. Before the tide comes in outside.

Time enough to open ti the curtains. Put the milk in the icebox. Rinse your coffee cup in the sink. Make the dining room table disappear. Turn the full-length double bed into a seat. And that's it.

You're ready to head for higher ground in a VW-type station wagon with all the VW-type virtues.

A new 1972 engine that's 32% more powerful than ever before. And that's located in the rear for better traction in sand and snow. (We got you into this mess. And we'll get you out of it.)

Gas economy. In the grand old Volkswagen tradition.

And space. More than you'd get in any conventional station wagon.

So if you go home empty-handed in a Campmobile, you're really empty.

The 60 mph motel.

While the average motel is all very nice in its place, it has a monotonous habit of staying in its place.

You don't have to put up with that.

With a VW Campmobile, you can always leave the place you're in without ever leaving the lodgings you're in. The lodgings go where you go.

Up to the loftiest mountain tops. Into the deepest forests.

Although the lodgings aren't exactly plush, they're very cozy. You'll find a full-length double bed, a child's bed, a hammock and a cot. As well as closets, curtains, worktables and a reading lamp.

There's even a kitchenette. Complete with a cupboard, a dining table, an icebox and a sink.

The complete cost (including the optional pop-up top and tent) is $3,382.*

Cheap for a car that'll take you down life's highways.

Ridiculous for a motel that'll take you down life's highways.

Instead of a second car, get a second house.

It's not as expensive as it sounds. There's no land to buy. No real-estate taxes to pay. Yet you can own a hunting lodge in the mountains. Or a cottage at the beach. And you won't need a car to get you there.

All you need is a Volkswagen Campmobile which, as houses go, is rather unusual. It goes.

But most people buy the Campmobile for what it comes with. Kitchen including sink, icebox and water pump. Dining table. Bedroom enough for two adults and two kids. Closets. Screens. Curtains.

Add the optional pop-up top and tent and the cost of this home-away-from-home is $3,290.*

Lots of people pay that much for a car. And some pay that much for a vacation.

But very few pay that little for a house.

This is an ad for the Volkswagen Station Wagon.

As you can see, this wagon is loaded with reasons for owning a Volkswagen Station Wagon.

There's too much stuff, and not enough wagon. Only about 85 cubic feet worth.

If you owned a box-shaped VW, you could take all that stuff off the roof and put it inside where it belongs.

The VW holds 170 cubic feet; about twice as much as most regular wagons.

Or you can seat 9 people and still have room for all their luggage.

Aside from capacity, you also get a sensible little engine that averages 23 miles on a gallon of regular.

And you never have to pay for anti-freeze, hoses or radiator repair.

There isn't any radiator.

So every time they make a conventional station wagon, they also make a swell little ad for the Volkswagen Station Wagon.

(Secretly, we wish them every success.)

152

Doyle Dane Bernbach Inc.

1

Open on VW Camper parked in
deserted desert landscape.

MVO: A Volkswagen Campmobile
can take you away from it all.

2

To a new, more quiet world where
few families have ever been.

SFX: Monster roaring.

As monster emerges from behind
rock film speeds up and family
pack into camper and drive off.

3

MVO: And when things become too
quiet, in less than five minutes
a Volkswagen campmobile can
turn into a station wagon.

4

And take you away from it all.

Desert Monster

Volkswagen presents the United States of America.

Climb into a VW Campmobile, turn the key and you have the entire country at your disposal.

You want the mountains? The VW Campmobile is an awesome mountain climber. Since the engine's in the rear, you get such good traction you don't even need a road.

You want snow country? You can have snow country. Since the engine's air cooled, you can travel in even the iciest weather and never have to worry about water or anti-freeze.

You just want to ride from town to town (or around town)? Then ride. A gallon of gas will take you about 23 miles.

Of course, wherever you settle in this land, you'll settle in comfort.

The VW Campmobile has a big full length double bed, a child's bed and a hammock.

It also has a kitchenette. Complete with a dining table, a sink, an icebox and a water system.

The price of the VW Campmobile is $2,931.*

America is free.

Doyle Dane Bernbach Inc.

1

Open on elderly couple timidly ringing apartment door bell.

Old Man: Are you the people with the Station wagon?

The one that holds twice as much as any other station wagon.

2

Husband: Tell him we're eating.

Old Man: But we've come so far.

3

Old Man: That's it, dear. The Volkswagen station wagon. The one that holds about twice as much as the average station-wagon.

4

Old Man: Thank you.

SFX: Doorbell ringing.

Elderly Couple

Open on man driving up to border
in VW Stationwagon.

Chinese guards collapse in
laughter until they look inside.

A sergeant reprimands guards
and sends driver back.

Senior Officer: Wasn't that
one of those Volkswagen
Stationwagons that holds twice
as much as any of our wagons.

Sergeant: Yes, it was.

Senior Officer: You did the
right thing.

Red China

The Karmann Ghia.

Designed by the Ghia design studio in Turin and coachbuilt by Karmann of Osnabruck, the Karmann Ghia looked every inch a racy Italian sports car.

The only drawback was that its sleek lines concealed the mechanical components, and hence the performance, of the standard Volkswagen Beetle.

Why Volkswagen could never make a body like this.

We'd be out of our minds.

Every seam in this car is welded by hand. Then ground down.

Filed.

Sanded with emery paper.

All by hand. You'd think one was all they were going to make.

And yet, that is a Volkswagen the man's working on.

The VW Karmann Ghia.

A posh little coupe for 2.

But we don't make this one ourselves. The hand work would bog us down.

We farm it out to one of Europe's last great coachworks, Karmann of Osnabrück. (It takes 185 men to make the body alone. If you're going to be posh, be posh.)

And yet, the engine, transmission and chassis are right out of our VW Sedan.

You get the legendary VW mileage. The VW air-cooled engine. The famous VW traction in snow, mud and sand.

And VW parts are all you ever need.

 The coupe's $2,295,* the convertible, $2,495.*

Anybody for an undercover Volkswagen?

The Volkswagen is the one in red.

These cars look alike to a Volkswagen mechanic.

They have the same engine, the same transmission, and the same chassis.

But the one on the bottom got mixed up with an Italian who thought our Volkswagen would make a sexy little runabout. Ghia of Turin.

The car's the VW Karmann Ghia.

Its special body takes so much hand work that we farm it out to one of Europe's greatest custom coachworks, Karmann of Osnabrück. Every seam is welded, ground down, filed and sanded by hand.

It's been mistaken for everything from a Ferrari to a Lancia.

Yet VW parts are all you need.

You get the VW's legendary mileage.

VW's air-cooled engine. And the famous Volkswagen traction in snow and sand.

Along with a gee-gaw or two. A defroster for the back window. Acoustical soundproofing. Adjustable bucket seats.

The price is quite a coup for a coupe like this. Hardtop, $2,295.* Convertible, $2,495.* Hardly an arm and a leg.

1

Open on very plain young couple
in suburban sitting room.

MVO: Will John ever get a
chance to be alone with Evelyn?
Will Evelyn ever find out if
she really loves John?

2

Will Evelyn's mother ever find
out three's a crowd?

The Volkswagen people give
them a chance to find the
answers.

John: Would you like to go for
a ride?

3

Evelyn's mother: I'll get my
hat.

MVO: That chance is the Karmann
Ghia. It has an economical
dependable Volkswagen engine
in a racy, romantic, hand
finished body.

4

But best of all, instead of
having seats for four, the
Karmann Ghia only has seats for
two.
Only two.

Mother in Law

Mechanic: We ought to have a new transmission, Mr. Potts. As soon as the mail strike's over. In Italy.

Mr. Potts: But I just bought it.

Dissolve to same scene sometime later.

Mechanic: The carburettor's got some grit stuck in its throat.

Dissolve again.

Mechanic: What can I tell you, Mr. Potts.

MVO: If someone else is spending more time with your sports car than you are, get an advanced sports car as reliable as a Volkswagen. A Volkswagen Karmann Ghia.

Mr. Potts

Can you spot the Volkswagen?

Lost among five of the world's great sports cars is one of the world's great Volkswagens.

The VW Karmann Ghia.

If you confuse it with a 170 mph sports machine, we wouldn't be surprised.

The racy lines are the work of a famous sports car designer, the Ghia studios of Turin, Italy.

And the bodywork is the handiwork of one of Europe's oldest custom coachmakers, Karmann of Osnabrück.

What makes the Karmann Ghia a Volkswagen is everything that makes it go. Independent 4-wheel suspension that takes curves like a racer. Surprisingly smooth 4-speed gear box. And an air-cooled engine that averages up to 28 mpg.

Of course, you can't reach the speed of a $15,000 Ferrari (top left), a $16,000 Lamborghini (top center), a $9,000 Mercedes Benz (top right), a $15,000 Maserati (bottom center), or a $14,000 Aston Martin (bottom right) in a Karmann Ghia (bottom left).

But it costs only $2,250* to give the impression that you can.

Volkswagen Karmann Ghia

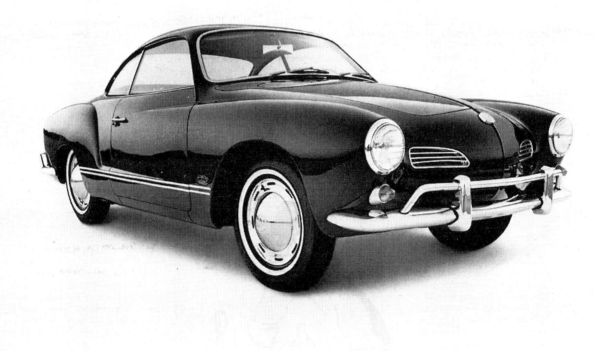

There's a little bug in every Karmann Ghia.

Underneath it all, this fancy hunk of car is still a Volkswagen.

It's got Volkswagen's 4-speed synchro-mesh transmission. And the Volkswagen's chassis and torsion bar suspension.

The big wheels that rack up 40,000 and more miles on a set of tires are all VW.

And so is the air-cooled engine that can't boil over in the summer or freeze up in the winter.

32 miles on a gallon of regular and no oil between changes are practically s.o.p. on the Karmann Ghia.

Not to mention the remarkable Volks-wagen traction. The inexpensive and easy-to-come-by parts. The low insurance. The reasonably priced, reliable service.

You can't see the "bug" part of a Karmann Ghia because it's traveling in-cognito in a sporty, Italian-designed body.

 So you can drive a Karmann Ghia and most people won't even know it's got a bug in it.

But you will.

Volkswagen.

When you go to buy a Volkswagen, you have a choice: The plain stubby-nosed model. Or the Italian style model with the noble Roman nose.

The fancy Volkswagen-built-for-two is called the Karmann Ghia.

The Karmann Ghia has everything the plain Volks does:

Air-cooled rear engine. Synchromesh 4-speed transmission. Torsion bars on all four wheels.

It also has a body full of hand work.

The Ghia wasn't designed for mass production. So it doesn't get the mass production treatment.

We make it in an old-fashioned custom way.

Volkswagen.

Fenders, hoods and door frames are welded and shaped and smoothed by hand.

Seats and convertible tops are padded and stitched and fitted by hand.

Sitting in the Ghia, you might not think you're in a Volkswagen at all.

Until you feel that nice firm Volkswagen traction. Pay those pint-sized oil and gas bills. Get that phenomenal tire wear. And take in our inexpensive VW service.

Which only goes to show you, even a Volkswagen with a fancy body, and a noble Roman nose, is still a Volkswagen at heart.

166

With technological triumphs like this, it only takes 4½ hours for 2 men to make one Karmann Ghia convertible top.

It used to take longer, till we discovered that curved needles sew around corners faster than straight needles.

That's important to us, because we want to make cars as efficiently as possible. What slows us down is that we also want to make cars as good as possible.

For us to do that, a Karmann Ghia convertible comes out costing you $2445. Which sounds like a lot of money coming out of your pocket. Until you realize what we put into the car.

Our convertible top, for example, has a vinyl interior that covers up the cross braces you see in most other convertibles. It has a thick pad of insulation in the middle that keeps out heat, cold and noise. And it has a vinyl outside that really fits because we really hand-fit it.

We could skip all that handwork, trade in all our curved needles for a couple of machines, and make convertible tops as efficiently as everyone else.

But we'd rather be less efficient and better. Instead of just as efficient and not as good.

Volkswagen economy is standard equipment.

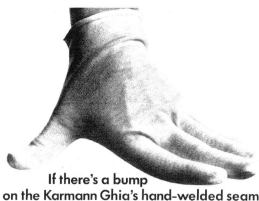

If there's a bump on the Karmann Ghia's hand-welded seams, this sensitive machine will find it.

We could use machines to look for mistakes. But machines don't care if they find them or not.

Our inspectors are only humans, but they're interested in what they find. And they don't just look for mistakes; they feel for them. (The white glove isn't a status symbol; it protects against calluses.)

So every last square inch of the Karmann Ghia body is sure to get the twice-over.

Including every seam (there are almost 20; try and find them); all four coats of paint (five on two-tone cars); all hand-sanding operations (even the inside of the glove compartment door); and the hand-finished interior (the seats, the insulated roof, the padded dash).

Our inspectors reject anything they don't like, and we cheerfully accept their rejection. All we ask is that they take pride in their work. Which is more than we can ask of a machine.

You just can't buy pride for any amount of money. But you can buy its product for only $2250.*

It does everything like a Volkswagen except look ugly.

For people who can't stand the sight of a Volkswagen.

Some people just can't see a VW. Even though they admire its attributes, they picture themselves in something fancier.

We sell such a package.

It's called a Karmann Ghia.

The Karmann Ghia is what happened to a Volkswagen when an Italian designer got hold of it.

He didn't design it for mass production, so we wouldn't think of giving it the mass production treatment.

We take time to hand-weld, hand-shape, and hand-smooth the body.

Finally, after 185 men have had a hand in it, the Ghia's body is lowered onto one of those strictly functional chassis.

The kind that comes with VW's big 15-inch wheels, torsion bars, our 4-speed synchromesh transmission and that famous air-cooled engine.

So that along with its Roman nose and graceful curves, the Ghia has a beauty that is more than skin deep.

You'd lose.

The racy-looking car in the picture would have trouble beating a Volkswagen.

Because it is a Volkswagen. Inside.

Outside it's a Karmann Ghia.

A Karmann Ghia isn't really a racing car. Though it is custom-built like one.

Its lines are too sculptured for mass production.

The front fender, for instance, has to be formed in three sections.

Each section is welded together. Then ground down, filed and sanded. All by hand. But beneath that wanton exterior beats a heart of Volkswagen.

Same engine, same chassis, same transmission. Which means same reliability, some economy, same service.

We know a Ghia can't do much at the Sebring road races.

But it can cruise at 72, corner like a sports car, and hold the road like one.

And it might comfort you to know, you'd be driving the best-made loser on the track.

1

Open on helicopter shot of
VW Karmann Ghia speeding along
beach.

2

MVO: The Volkswagen Karmann
Ghia is the most economical
sports car you can buy.

3

The car fails to break through
paper hoop.

4

MVO: It's just not the most
powerful.

Paper Hoop

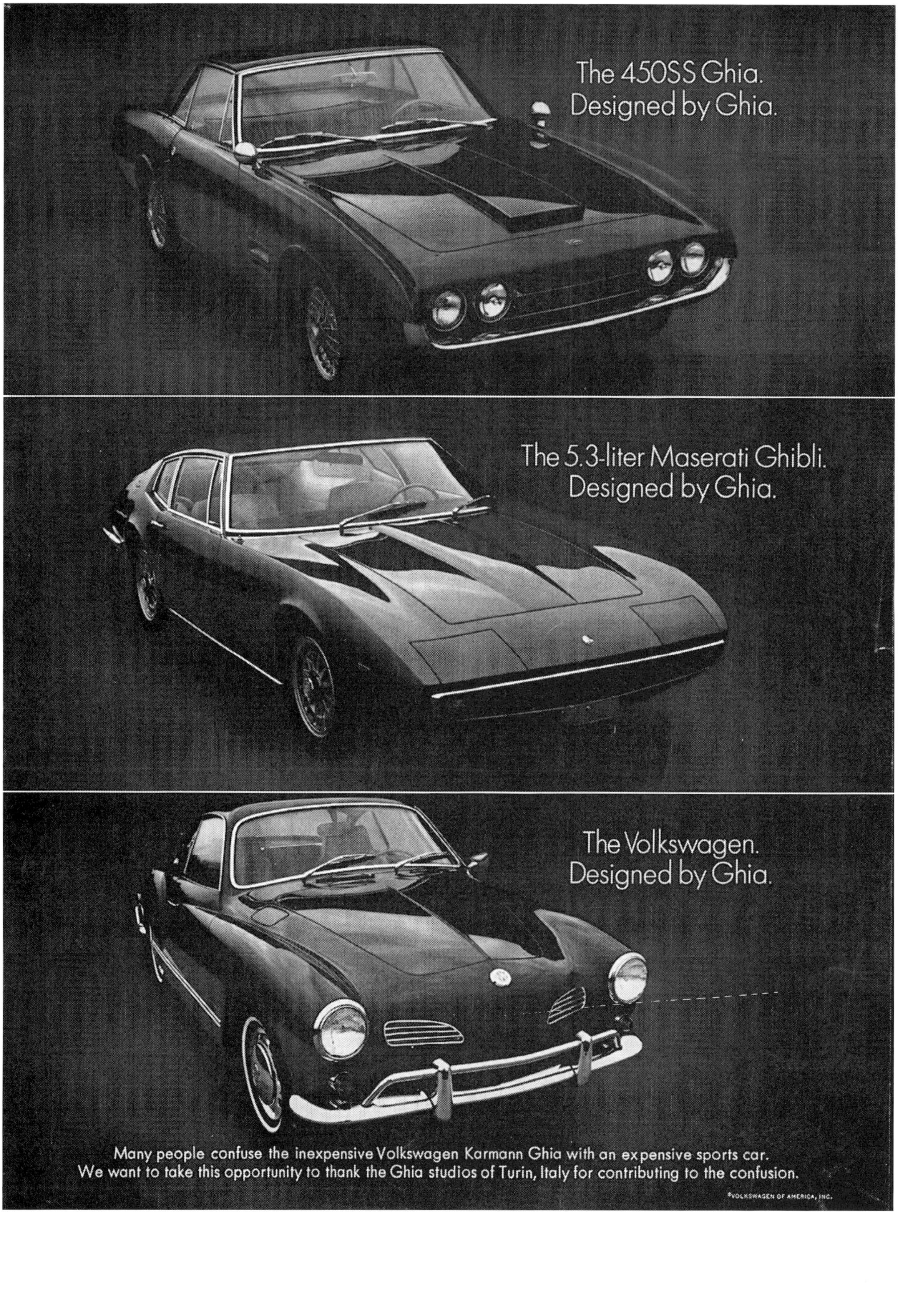
The 450SS Ghia.
Designed by Ghia.
The 5.3-liter Maserati Ghibli.
Designed by Ghia.
The Volkswagen.
Designed by Ghia.
Many people confuse the inexpensive Volkswagen Karmann Ghia with an expensive sports car.
We want to take this opportunity to thank the Ghia studios of Turin, Italy for contributing to the confusion.
©VOLKSWAGEN OF AMERICA, INC.

Can you spot the druggist from Toledo?

Of course not.

That's the point.

Somewhere in our picture is what appears to be just another Italian playboy sitting in his expensive Italian sports car.

But somewhere up there is a very dependable druggist in his very dependable Karmann Ghia.

It looks like a racy sports job because it was designed by the Ghia Studios of Turin, Italy.

It runs like a Volkswagen because, underneath, that's exactly what it is.

Complete with 4-wheel independent suspension, front disc brakes, 4-speed synchronized gear-box, oil cooler and rear-mounted air-cooled engine.

To put an end to the suspense, the Karmann Ghia is the snappy number just left of center.

And for a snappy $2,575*, it's yours. So you can look like the kind of person to whom price is no object.

And with the money you save, it won't be.

©VOLKSWAGEN OF AMERICA, INC. *SUGGESTED RETAIL PRICE, EAST COAST P.O.E. ($2,672 WEST COAST P.O.E.) LOCAL TAXES AND OTHER DEALER DELIVERY CHARGES, IF ANY, ADDITIONAL. WHITEWALLS OPTIONAL AT EXTRA COST.

The Fastback, the Squareback and the 411.

These cars extended Porsche's air-cooled, rear-engined concept up market, offering all the Beetle's traditional advantages, along with a bit more leg room and performance.

Low slung rear engines gave the the Fastback and Squareback an unusual feature - luggage compartments front and rear. While the extra power their engines produced enabled Volkswagen to pander to the American drivers' taste for fully automatic transmission for the first time.

The 411, an even roomier, faster and more luxurious saloon, was introduced to the USA in the early seventies. It met with only limited success and proved to be VW's last rear-engined design.

It has all the beauty of the ugly one.

A beautiful air-cooled motor that you don't have to worry about all winter, because it can't freeze. Beautifully situated in the rear of the car to make the traction better on sand, snow and ice.

Glamorous gas mileage (about 27 miles to the gallon). Voluptuous tire mileage (about 35,000 miles to the set).

Sensuous synchromesh transmission in all 4 forward gears, to make it shift smoothly.

Exotic independent suspension on all 4 wheels, to make it ride smoothly. (When one wheel goes over a bump it doesn't affect the opposite wheel.)

The VW Fastback also has a few additional charms all its own.

It goes a little faster. (84 mph.) And it gets up there a little faster. (0 to 70 mph in 28 seconds.)

There's a bit more room in the backseat of the Fastback than there is in the bug. And a good bit more trunk space. In fact, a whole extra trunkful.

It even costs more. ($XXXX*.)

But that's still nothing compared to cars that have most of their beauty where you can see it.

173

11 Extra Miles

Open 'er up and see what she can do.

Open the front where most compact sedans store an engine

You'll find our Type 3 stores luggage

Open the rear where most Volkswagens store an engine

You'll find our Type 3 stores luggage

Where's the engine?

Underneath the rear trunk. (For better traction.)

Where's the carburetor?

There isn't any carburetor.

Instead, our fuel-injected engine uses a little computer to measure out only the gas you absolutely need. (About 1 gallon for every 26 miles.)

What you won't have any trouble finding are the front disc brakes.

They're up front as standard equipment on every single Type 3 we make.

And there's no problem finding the

gears.

Since our stick shift is synchromesh, you can go through speeds 1,2,3, and 4 as easy as 1,2,3

Now one option you might consider is air conditioning.

So when hot air starts coming in, you have an alternative: To close 'er up and see what she can do.

Is anyone willing to take a chance?

Dear Reverend, Father or Rabbi:

We understand why you love to raffle off Cadillacs, T-Birds and Continentals.

They draw the crowds.

But consider the poor soul who wins.

He has to pay about $1000 in income tax. At least $425 a year for gas. And who knows how much for oil and antifreeze.

Now think how charitable it would be to raffle off a Volkswagen Fastback Sedan.

It needs only about $420 for income tax. About $150 a year for gas. No antifreeze. And, it takes pints of oil, not quarts.

Now you may ask, what makes this Volkswagen fancy enough to raffle off?

Well, it comes with wall-to-wall carpet-

ing. Front seats that adjust to 49 positions. Fold-down arm rests in the rear. An electric clock. And, as options: automatic transmission and air conditioning.

So, if you're thinking of raffling off a fancy car, lift up your eyes.

And behold.

The Volkswagen Fastback Sedan.

The Volkswagen Fastback

176

Doyle Dane Bernbach Inc.

1

Open on man standing by VW 1600
Fastback.

<u>Man:</u> If you've never bought a
Volkswagen because it wasn't big
enough, Okay.

Here's a Volkswagen that's big
enough.

The new VW fastback sedan.

2

It seats four with more room for
elbows and legs. It's pretty
jazzy too. Has an electric
clock and even wall to wall
carpeting.

The fastback also has the most
powerful engine we've ever made.

3

It's air cooled, goes 27 miles
on a gallon of gas which is
pretty good for a car that can
go 84 miles per hour.

Since we made a VW that's a
little roomier on the inside we
decided to do the same thing
on the outside.

4

It's got a trunk up front where
most cars have their motors and
in the back where most cars have
their trunks, we have a......

.....it's a trunk, large trunk.

<u>MVO:</u> Call in at your VW dealer.
He'll show you where the motor is.

Dustin Hoffman

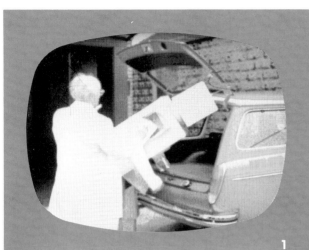

Doyle Dane Bernbach Inc.

1

Open on robot and scientist
leaving a building.

They approach VW Square-back.

2

The robot tries to get in the
back of VW.

3

MVO: If things don't all fit
in the back of the Volkswagen
Square-back Sedan, don't
worry.

4

Some things can fit in the
front.

Robot

Doyle Dane Bernbach Inc.

1

Open on Penguins walking
around.

<u>MVO:</u>

On a hot, muggy evening

2

when you're all dressed up to
go meet your friends and go
out on the town,

3

we just thought you'd be
interested to know

4

that all Volkswagens are now
available with air conditioning.

Penguins

Doyle Dane Bernbach Inc.

Open on two Russians at door of garage.

Inventor: Commisar Vishenzko. After all this time. After four, five year plans I have finally perfected perfect people's car.

In one car I am putting two cars. Is have all economy of little car and is have much capacity like bigger car. Is have engine in the rear - is air cooled.

Commisar: Comrade. . .

In one car, is put two cars. Is have all economy of little car and is have much capacity like bigger car. Is have engine in rear, is air cooled.

Is already has been perfected perfect people's car. Is called Volkswagen Square-back Sedan.

Come Comrade, we take you for little ride.

Russian Inventor

Doyle Dane Bernbach Inc.

Open on dawn breaking in
pretty mid western landscape.

MVO:

The day began as every other
day had begun. But then a
strange stillness fell over
the land and a sound was heard
in the distance.

It was coming. And the people
sensed it, and were glad. And
when they saw it they could
not believe it. A Volkswagen.

Unlike any other Volkswagen.
Big with four big doors.

And all the comfort of a big
car. With a powerful engine
and electronic fuel injection.
And an automatic transmission,
all of which the people did not
pay extra for.

After all these years a big car
as good as a Volkswagen.
And the people rejoiced.
The Volkswagen 411 4-door Sedan
had come.

SFX:

Angelic choir.

It's Coming

© VOLKSWAGEN OF AMERICA, INC.

It can save you an arm and a leg.

Two ways.

First, our automatic transmission* means no more shifting or clutching in a VW.

It makes driving a Volkswagen as easy as stepping on the gas.

Second, when you do step on the gas, it makes your touch a light one.

Because while the average automatic transmission gets a lowly 15 mpg, ours gets about 25.

After a year (or 12,000 miles), that saves you over $100 on gas alone.

You'll find our automatic transmission in both the VW Squareback and Fastback.

Join the Volkswagen automatic savings plan.

*optional

The idea behind the Volkswagen Squareback Sedan.

Twenty-three years ago, we had an idea for a small economy car.

And it came out looking like a bug.

Twenty years ago, we had an idea for a giant station wagon.

And it came out looking like a box.

Then we had an idea for a sedan that combined all the economy of our bug with a lot of the capacity of our box.

So you'd expect it to come out looking half bug, half box. Right?

Wrong.

Our Squareback Sedan looks like a small station wagon.

But by squaring off its back and adding a trunk in front, our little sedan can give you over twice as much carrying space as the biggest domestic sedan.

Years ago, we learned the important thing isn't the way a car looks on the outside, but how it works on the inside.

And so it's just as true today as it was then: You can't judge a Volkswagen by its cover.

Doyle Dane Bernbach Inc.

1

Open on King Kong on top of
Empire State Building.

<u>MVO</u>: If you've been looking
high and low for a big car as
good as a Volkswagen, maybe you
should look into our big car,
the Volkswagen 411.

2

It has some things no VW ever
had. Like four big doors and
lots of room and luxury for
the whole family. It has
some advanced things most
other cars don't have.

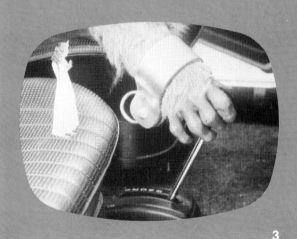

3

Like electronic fuel-injection,
an automatic pre-heating system
and a big trunk up front.
But you don't have to be a
genius to drive the 411 because
it comes with automatic transmission as standard equipment.

4

So now there's a Volkswagen
big enough for just about
everyone.

The VW411 Four door sedan.

King Kong

VW advertising outside
the USA.

Following the amazing success of the campaign in the States, Doyle Dane Bernbach was asked to handle the VW account in several other countries.

This is just a small proportion of the outstanding · advertising that has been created in the agency's offices outside the USA.

"Les docteurs, nous on n'y croit pas."

A la campagne, il faut être solide. Les hommes sont durs au travail, ils n'ont jamais besoin des docteurs, ni de leurs pilules. Les bêtes vêlent toutes seules sans vétérinaire. Et l'auto dans la cour ne doit pas avoir besoin de garagiste. Comme la Coccinelle.

La Coccinelle peut bien passer la nuit dehors, elle ne tousse jamais le matin.

C'est normal, avec un moteur refroidi par air, qui n'utilise ni eau ni antigel, on démarre par tous les temps.

Elle est résistante. Depuis le temps qu'elle va aux champs tous les jours, elle a bien fait 2 fois le tour de la terre. Sans jamais lever le capot.

Et puis elle est robuste. Avec ses 34 CV elle a remorqué le tracteur jusqu'à la ferme plus d'une fois. Et sa suspension est à l'épreuve des ornières les plus profondes.

Et sobre, avec ça. Une vidange tous les 5 000 km seulement, un peu d'essence de temps en temps... Dame, faut ce qu'il faut.

Bien sûr elle a pris quelques bosses. Mais l'important, c'est qu'elle fasse son travail tous les jours. Tant qu'on a la santé...

All for the price of an Austin 1100.

Whats the catch?

There isn't any.

The Austin 1100 costs £740.*

The Volkswagen 1200 costs £685.

Which leaves you £55 to spend if you buy the Volkswagen.

The fridge was £49.19.6. from Selfridges.

The roof-rack, £4.19.6. And the rope (second-hand) we valued at one shilling.

So for the same money as the Austin you not only get a Volkswagen but a few extras on top.

Running a Volkswagen won't run away with your money, either.

You should get about 38 miles to a gallon and 40,000 miles to a set of tyres.

Maybe a little more. Maybe a little less. Depending on how you drive.

As far as the Volkswagen engine goes, its been known to go a very long way, indeed.

Mr. T. Levy of 18, Abbotsbury Gardens, Eastcote, recently told us of a VW engine that clocked up over 350,000 miles.

All of which makes the Volkswagen a pretty good buy.

Even if you don't need a fridge.

You can spot one a mile off.

We're happy to say the Volkswagen still looks like nothing on earth.

Except another Volkswagen.

And in an age where cars are getting to look more and more alike, isn't that refreshing?

Not that we made the VW different just to be different.

Our bonnet is short and stubby because it helps the driver see where he's going.

Our wheels are big because that helps tyre wear.

VW owners often get 40,000 to a set.

And a lot of cars are just catching on to the aerodynamics of our sloping roof.

Some of our styling advantages you can't even see from the outside.

Like the leg room.

Because we don't have an engine in the front, there's room for legs in the front.

Or like the big space we have behind the back seat.

Big enough to sleep a baby. It'll take other bundles, too.

The point is when you buy a Volkswagen you don't just get a car that looks different.

You get a car that looks different for a reason.

It'll be nice when it's finished.

For us, the event that crowned coronation year was the arrival of the Volkswagen.

We thought it was a car that could never be improved.

Next year we improved it.

Not to make it better-looking.

But to make it better-working.

The year after we did it again.

It's been the same story every year since.

A bigger engine here. A bigger window there.

An automatic choke.

A dual braking system.

Unfortunately for the nostalgic, there's hardly a part on the VW that's escaped some technical advance or other.

In fact, right this very moment we're using this year's model to practise on for next year's.

And you know what practice makes.

It makes your tyres go farther.

The little gadget in the photograph is called a Volkswagen.

When fitted to tyres it can have a remarkable effect on their longevity.

The secret lies in the size of the wheels.

The Volkswagen has 15" wheels. While most cars have only 13" wheels.

So over a given distance the VW wheels go round fewer times.

Which gives the tyres less opportunity to wear out.

Ingenious.

Mr James T Morrison of Knightswood Road, Glasgow, recently wrote to us on this very subject.

"It may interest you to know that on my 1961 Volkswagen my reading at this date is 58,244 miles. And I still have almost 3mm on each tyre."

So while our big wheels may not seem such a big deal in the showroom, the longer you keep your Volkswagen the more revolutionary the idea gets.

To close the door, open the window.

Shutting a door on a Volkswagen can be pretty frustrating if you don't handle it right.

The harder you slam it, the faster it jumps open again.

This happens because Volkswagens are made in a way that's almost forgotten these days.

Well.

Parts that are supposed to fit other parts fit them.

Parts that aren't, don't.

And instead of spot welding, we bolt the chassis onto the body. Fitting a continuous rubber seal between the two.

Consequently, the VW is not only watertight but practically airtight.

So when you try to shut the door, you can trap too much air inside.

What you have to do then is let some of it out. By opening a window first. (The merest crack will be enough.)

Naturally, we could have made things easier for you.

But we didn't.

It would have meant making this VW worse.

Eigenartig.

Eigenartig schon, wie wir anfangen, unseren Motor zu bauen. Das Metall für die Motorblock-Legierung kommt aus dem Wasser. Magnesium. Magnesium ist leicht. (Der ganze Motor wiegt ganze 105 kg.) Magnesium ist widerstandsfähig.

Eigenartig dann, wie wir die Zylinder anordnen. Um Platz zu sparen, legen wir alle 4 flach. Je 2 und 2 gegenüber. Deshalb nennt man den VW-Motor Boxer-Motor. (Und es dauert lange, ihn k.o. zu bekommen.)

Eigenartig auch, wo wir ihn einbauen. Hinten. Statt vorn. Da braucht er keine Kardanwelle. Motor und Getriebe sind in einem Paket. Direkt bei den Antriebsrädern. Eigenartig schließlich, womit wir ihn kühlen. Mit Luft. Statt Wasser. Luft friert nie ein und kocht nie über.

 Was eigenartig an ihm sein kann, ist eigenartig. Das macht ihn zum Motor eigener Art.

What are you d

If you're not doing anything special (again), you might like to consider this piece of sheer escapism from Volkswagen.

It's called the Volkswagen Continental.

(That's it on the right hand page.)

It's a simple device that, with the turn of a key,

can transport you, your family, your dog and all your home comforts anywhere you care to go.

You can cook in it. There's a stainless steel cooker and wash basin.

Eat in it. In just a few folds, travelling room for six becomes a neat little dining room.

g this weekend?

And sleep in it. A few more folds turn the dining room into a double bed for you, and a couple of extra beds for the kids.

There's even a cupboard and a wardrobe.

And it's all tucked away in a body only 14" longer than a Beetle.

But if you're worried about the kids getting on top of you, we'd like to add that the Continental comes with its own home extension:

A 6'6"x9'8" free-standing tent.

Pitch it wherever your fancy takes you.

Home is where your Continental is.

It's possible.

As far as we know, nobody has ever bought a Volkswagen because of its speed.

Its virtues have always been of the more homely kind.

An air-cooled engine that can't boil or freeze.

A paintwork job that can stay out all night and never show it.

A shape that doesn't go out of style every year, leaving the owner out of pocket.

As a result, the VW has a great image as a practical car.

And practically no image as a performance car.

And we do have a story:

The new 1500 c.c. VW does 78 mph. Fast enough to get copped for speeding on any road in the country.

In fact, in the long run, the VW can prove faster than many faster cars.

Its engine is so low-revving, it's virtually impossible to over-work it. So its top speed is also its cruising speed.

It'll go flat out, all day. From the very day you drive it out of the showroom.

Volkswagens don't need running-in.

Though the police have been known to disagree.

VOLKSWAGEN MOTORS LIMITED VOLKSWAGEN HOUSE PURLEY SURREY TELEPHONE: 01-668 4100

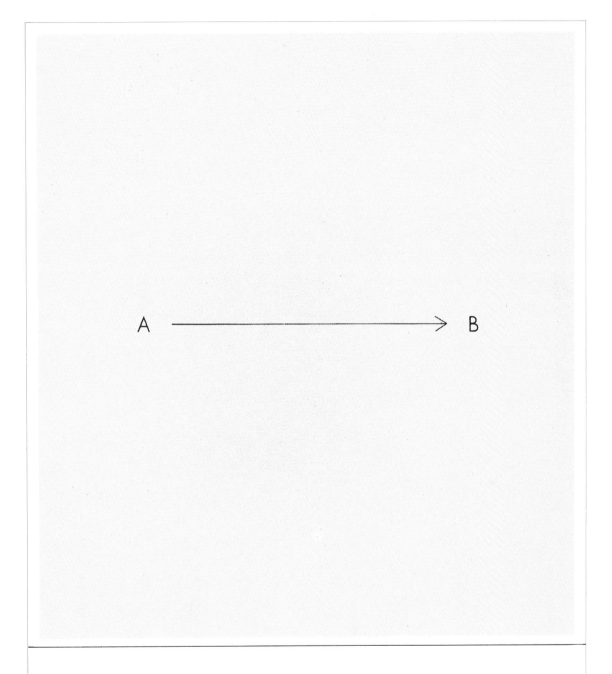

We can do it cheaper than most.

If the cost of getting from A to B is beginning to get you down, maybe its time you bought a Volkswagen.

At £685, the Volkswagen 1200 is quite a bargain to start with.

And that's only the start.

You should get about 38 miles from a gallon of petrol. (Depending on how and where you drive.)

And since the VW runs very happily on the low-octane kind, that's 38 at 6/3d. a gallon, not 38 at 6/7d.

(Read on, it gets better.)

The VW uses very little oil.

And you'll never have to pay a penny for anti-freeze, or radiator repairs.

Because there isn't any radiator.

Tyres have been known to roll on for 40,000 miles.

Engines for much, much longer.

And there's no car around with a better reputation for re-sale value.

Your local VW dealer will be glad to arrange a test-drive. And to quote you on your present car.

Always assuming, of course, you can afford to drive it down there.

VOLKSWAGEN MOTORS LIMITED VOLKSWAGEN HOUSE PURLEY SURREY TELEPHONE: 01-668 4100

194

C'est bien, ma sœur,
de ne pas gaspiller l'argent de la paroisse.

De nos jours, la Coccinelle est un merveilleux placement pour l'argent des fidèles.

Ainsi les économies réalisées sur l'entretien (la Coccinelle ne nécessite qu'une vidange tous les 5.000 km et n'utilise ni eau ni antigel) pourront aller à l'orphelinat par exemple.

L'argent des réparations (une Coccinelle accomplit allègrement 100.000 km sans le moindre incident mécanique) sera peut-être consacré au clocher de l'église qui en a tellement besoin, lui.

Et pensons à la joie de nos chers vieux devant leurs étrennes. Puisque cette année encore, le prix de la Volkswagen 1200 ne change pas : 6980 F.

De tous temps le clergé français a su montrer l'exemple.

Et rouler en Coccinelle, c'est prêcher l'économie, la robustesse, la sécurité et même la modestie (la Coccinelle est si discrète).

Mais rouler en Coccinelle c'est également prêcher des convaincus.

Car nous avons aussi nos fidèles (plus de 12 millions de Coccinelles vendues dans le monde entier).

De toute façon, qui viendra dire aujourd'hui, avec ses nouvelles couleurs vives, que la Coccinelle est ennuyeuse comme un sermon ?

Will your car ever live to see it?

To stand any sort of chance, it needs a few things it probably hasn't got.

It needs a slow-revving engine (like a Volkswagen's).

One that hits top speed comfortably at only 4000 revs a minute instead of straining itself at the usual 5000 revs.

It needs a baked enamel finish (like a Volkswagen's).

To make sure its body doesn't crack up before its engine does.

And it needs a sealed bottom (like a Volkswagen's).

A one-piece steel plate that'll shut out dirt, rain, stones and salt, all the things

that can eat up a car.

With help like this, you should find it easier to stay the distance.

In fact, one car we know (a Volkswagen, as it happens) outlasted three engines. And clocked up over 600,000 miles.

And still it lives to tell the tale.

Why don't they ever sit on Volkswagens?

The only things we ever put on VWs are things that'll make them work better. And as yet, we haven't found any girls who could meet that small requirement.

So as usual at the Motor Show all our attractions are under our bonnets. Not on top.

For instance, the beauty of our new Super Beetle lies in an 85% bigger boot. And a new 1600cc engine that can cruise all day at 80mph.

Our 1600 Fastback and Variant now have electronic fuel injection. (At about half the price of other cars with similar systems.)

While our 1200cc Beetle features another eleven sensible improvements. And still costs under £700.

Granted, these attractions may seem a little dull alongside girls in bikinis.

But at least you can take them with you when you take the car.

Sometimes, it's nice not to have your name in the newspapers.

Visitez les vieilles cités médiévales,
grâce au nouveau rayon de braquage de la Coccinelle.

Passez une des portes d'enceinte, et prenez sans crainte les ruelles sinueuses.

Malgré les tournants aigus, les bornes, et les trois mètres de large des rues moyenâgeuses, le nouveau rayon de braquage de la Coccinelle (4,50 mètres) vous permettra de passer par les voies les plus étroites.

Et d'aller vous garer Place du Marché.

Achetez-y foies, confits, liqueurs, puisque la 1302 a un coffre de 260 litres.

De quoi emporter assez de provisions pour passer l'hiver.

Ouvrez tout grand les quatre bouches d'aération de la nouvelle climatisation si vous avez pris chaud en escaladant les 439 marches des remparts.

Et si vous avez pris froid dans les oubliettes, réchauffez-vous en ouvrant les neuf bouches de chauffage.

Mais surtout, ne vous hâtez pas dans les ruelles médiévales à la recherche du temps perdu. Sur l'autoroute, vous pourrez le rattraper à 135 km/h, puisque la puissance de la Coccinelle est passée de 34 à 44 CV DIN.

Il y a 25 ans que nous construisons la coccinelle. Et que nous la perfectionnons d'année en année.

Et si nous pensons aujourd'hui qu'elle est presque parfaite, c'est aussi pour circuler dans les villes du XXe siècle.

"No sir, it's only a test drive, you don't have to buy it.

Why don't you slip into the driving seat while I go round the other side.

Now, close the door. No try it again. No, you'll have to wind the window down a bit first. Everything fits so well the car's virtually airtight.

Turn the ignition. Yes, the engine is on. It's a lot quieter than you thought, isn't it?
I said it's a lot quieter than you thought isn't it?

No, there's no choke, it's built in. Okay, put it into gear and we'll go out into the traffic.

Notice the synchromesh on first? Into second. You're right. You can see a lot of the road. That sloping bonnet really helps.

Up to third. How do you feel so far?

Oh, I'm sure nobody's staring at you, sir. We've been selling this car for 19 years, it doesn't look unusual any more.

All right, let's go into top and move into the outside lane. Take your hands off the wheel for a second. See how steady the steering is.

Let's take the next left. Not cramped for leg room are you? Good. And for a man of your height—6′2″ is it?—you've still got room to wear a hat.

Well, it's nice to know you could if you wanted to, isn't it?

Pardon? Yes, the sun visors, screen-washers and heater are all standard fittings. You really know your specifications.

Now, straight down the road.

You didn't see those traffic lights? No, I just thought it would have been a good chance to try out the brakes that's all.

All right sir, why don't we try it a little faster. Take it right up to seventy. Ease up a little round this bend. Notice how the independent suspension kept the car nice and steady.

It is fun, but I think we ought to slow down a little while we're on the round-about. Good.

Okay sir, we're home. Just turn into the forecourt there and park by that low wall.

That's a little closer than I meant, sir. No, it's really all right, don't worry.

One of the nice things about Volkswagens is they're easy to fix. We'll have a new wing on in just about an hour.

Really, it's just a matter of taking 15 bolts off and putting 15 bolts on. No sweat.

Now, would you like to talk a little more in the office?

Fine. You have a car you'd like us to take in part exchange?

It's a 1952 Jowett Javelin? I see. And you were hoping for around £300?

There isn't a big demand for them you know…

Certainly, new seat covers are important, but… look let's go in the office and talk it over…"

 Your Volkswagen dealer is ready to give you a trial drive. Without fear or favour. Take him up on it.

£196.

If you can afford this much of a new Volkswagen you could be free to drive off with the rest.

Because you're putting down 25% of the £783 cash price.

And from now on, that's all your VW dealer asks of you.

He'll be happy to fix up a loan on the other 75%. As well as giving you three years to pay it back.

Of course, you may think that for a paltry sum like this, you can't be getting much of a car.

But on a VW, you get things you don't get on far more expensive cars.

An oil cooler for instance. Torsion bar suspension. A sealed bottom. And three coats of paint.

And once you get a VW on the road, there's no telling how much it'll save you in oil, petrol and repair bills.

 In fact, while you're paying for the rest of your VW, it's as good as paying for itself.

You can't buy one so new.

Now that we've got a decent back window, there's room enough to stick a running-in sign in.

But you'll never see one.

Because Volkswagens never need running in.

We put them together too intricately to leave room for that. (Any piston more than 1/1000th of a millimetre out, is out.)

What kind of a tolerance is that to be rounded off, we round off at the factory.

We bench-run every engine at 2,500 revs. Flushing out all the metal shavings with clean oil.

(It's a job you usually take your first 500 miles to do.)

After that, there are three more tests to do through.

The timing test. For camshaft and timing.

The function test. To check petrol adjustment and oil leaks.

And the performance test. Just to satisfy ourselves that the engine's slow enough to be a true Volkswagen.

VWs are slow running, remember, a new one.

Only when an engine's passed these tests is it passed on to you.

If we didn't put our test down in our factory, you wouldn't be able to put yours down as soon as you get in the car.

If you'd like to drive a VW, contact Volkswagen Motors Ltd, Volkswagen House, Purley, Surrey, CR2 2UQ.
Tel. 01-668 4100. We'll put you in touch with your nearest dealer.

Dissimulez vos bénéfices.

Nous savons bien que vous ne fraudez pas le fisc.

Et que vous êtes un bon Français.

Tenez, nous pensons même que l'idée ne vous en est jamais venue.

Mais de là à faire étalage de vos moyens.

A montrer que vous gagnez beaucoup d'argent. Enfin assez d'argent.

A attirer l'attention sur vos revenus.

Non.

Et nous vous comprenons très bien.

C'est pourquoi nous avons voulu que la Coccinelle soit si discrète.

Sans tapage. Sans chrome et sans clinquant inutile.

Prenons un exemple : nous n'avons pas mis 50 compteurs.

Il n'y a rien à surveiller.

Tout ce qu'on peut dire de vous quand vous roulez en Coccinelle, c'est que vous êtes intelligent.

Intelligent d'avoir choisi une voiture aussi robuste, aussi économique, aussi sûre.

Une voiture qui coûte si peu à l'achat, et tellement à la revente.

Une voiture qui ne demande pas d'entretien, et qui parcourt 100 000 km sans problèmes.

Vous pouvez rouler en Coccinelle et personne ne pourra dire combien vous gagnez.

On pourra tout juste dire combien vous réfléchissez.

Et ça, même votre percepteur ne pourra vous le reprocher.

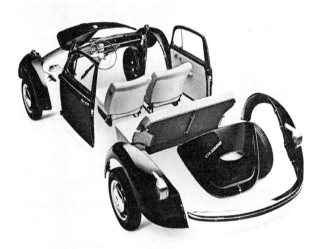

Das haben wir diesmal verbessert.

Alles, was Sie da sehen, haben wir in diesem Herbst am VW 1300 und am VW 1500 verbessert. Und einiges, was Sie nicht sehen können.

Es ist mehr als je zuvor.

Ein gutes Dutzend Verbesserungen ist allein dazu da, den Käfer noch sicherer zu machen.

Zum Beispiel die Zweikreis-Bremsanlage. Die auch dann noch funktioniert, wenn eines der beiden Leitungssysteme ausfallen sollte. (Was Sie wohl kaum erleben werden.)

Und die Sicherheitslenksäule. Das Sicherheitslenkrad. Die neuen Scheinwerfer mit senkrechten Streuscheiben. Die Scheibenwischer mit zwei Geschwindigkeiten. Die Sicherheitsspiegel innen und außen. Die breiteren, stärkeren und höher angebrachten Stoßstangen.

Auch für den Komfort haben wir einiges getan.

Die angenehmste Neuerung ist zweifellos die Frischluftbelüftung. Sie können die Luftzufuhr an zwei Knöpfen getrennt für links und rechts regeln. Und brauchen nicht mehr den lauten und zugigen Fahrtwind durch das Fenster hereinzulassen.

Neu ist auch, daß man jetzt die Beifahrertür auf- und zuschließen kann.

Und daß man zum Tanken nicht mehr die vordere Haube zu öffnen braucht: Der Tankeinfüllstutzen ist jetzt außen rechts hinter einer Federklappe.

Was nicht neu ist, ist der Preis. Die beiden Käfer kosten keinen Pfennig mehr als bisher.

Ist das nicht auch eine hübsche Verbesserung?

It comes apart quicker than most.

A VW may not be the fastest thing on the road, but it may well be the fastest off it.

On the odd occasions when something needs fixing, it's a quick and simple job.

Our mechanics can whip out an engine in 45 minutes flat. And slip a new one back just as smartly.

They don't need overtime to replace a transmission unit either. (The way they would on a lot of cars.)

2½ hours should see them through.

Part time for installing a clutch is 1 hour 20 minutes. For replacing and adjusting a carburettor: just 20 minutes.

Even something as nasty as a dented wing is soon back in shape again.

In three hours they can have a shiny new one painted, wired up and bolted on. No sweat.

Which is why if your VW ever runs into trouble, it won't cost the earth to put it right.

Since our mechanics don't spend long on the job, you don't spend much on them.

Auf Ihren VW kann sich Ihr Nachbar verlassen.

Vielleicht hat er manchmal ein bißchen hochmütig über Ihren Käfer gelächelt. Aber im Winter ist er froh, daß Sie in der Nähe wohnen.

Genießen Sie diesen Triumph diskret.

Lassen Sie ihn nicht allzu deutlich spüren, was Sie von einem Auto halten, das nicht, wie der VW, eine Startautomatik hat.

Das nicht, wie der VW, mit Luft, sondern mit Wasser gekühlt wird. Und deswegen einen Wasserkühler und eine Wasserpumpe hat, die einfrieren können.

Das nicht, wie der VW, einen Motor hat, der mit seinem ganzen Gewicht auf die Antriebsräder drückt und es ihnen somit schwer macht, durchzudrehen.

Das nicht, wie der VW, eine völlig dichte Boden-platte hat. Die so empfindliche Dinge wie die Benzinleitung und die Bremsleitung schützt.

Streuen Sie nicht Salz in seine Wunden. (Sondern auf die Fahrbahn.) Helfen Sie ihm, sein Auto wieder flottzukriegen. Denn wer weiß, ob Sie ihn nicht eines Tages auch mal brauchen.

Bei einem Plattfuß vielleicht.

A Volkswagen for people who can't afford to be seen in a Volkswagen.

It's the Volkswagen 411.

But it doesn't look like a Volkswagen.

So you won't have to worry about keeping up appearances.

It comes with more doors than a Volkswagen. (One conveniently placed near the driving seat for a chauffeur.)

It's got more luggage room than a Volkswagen. 20 cubic feet in all.

And more comfort.

The front seat can be adjusted to any of 400 positions.

There's more speed. (It'll cruise all day at 90 mph.)

And a lot of refinement. Rubber bumpers. A dual braking system. A double-jointed rear axle. (Just like on a Porsche.)

Not to mention a heater you can leave on when you leave the car.

But the big advantage is price.

The 411 costs considerably more than a Volkswagen.

The four-door version in the picture goes for £1282.

But with automatic transmission, and other extras, you should be able to push it up to almost £1600.

Of course, like all Volkswagens, it holds its value very well.

But you needn't tell the neighbours that.

Let them think it's just another fancy foreign car you're going to lose a packet on.

VOLKSWAGEN MOTORS LIMITED VOLKSWAGEN HOUSE PURLEY SURREY TELEPHONE: 01-668 4100

Some of the silly questions you get asked when you own a Volkswagen 411 LE Estate.

1. "What is it?"

Not everyone guesses right away that it's a Volkswagen.

They think because it looks big and fancy, it must have a big fancy name.

If you'd rather they went on thinking that, you're not obliged to answer the question.

2. "Where's the engine?"

Apparently, it doesn't have one.

At the front, it has a boot (size 14·1 cu.ft.). At the back, it has another boot (size 24·7 cu.ft.).

And if you push the back seat forward, all you find is another 24·1 cu.ft. of empty space.

However, if you have to let someone into the secret, lift up the floor of the rear luggage compartment.

All will be revealed.

3. "How does it work without a carburettor?"

The short answer is that it has something much smarter: an electronic fuel injection system.

A computer absorbs information from sensors fitted to your engine. Then works out precisely how much fuel each cylinder needs for its next stroke.

This way, less power goes to waste; maximum power comes from the engine.

For example: 0-50 mph in 10·5 seconds, cruising speed 96 mph.

4. "Where do I put the petrol in?"

No one gets to the filler system without your say so.

Direct them round to the front offside wing. And open the filler cap from inside the car.

5. "Now you've turned off the engine, what's that funny noise?"

Don't panic.

It's just the heater still churning out heat.

It doesn't rely on the engine you see. So you can run it even when you're parked.

It's thermostatically controlled too. Which means it'll work up to a chosen temperature without ever working up a fug.

6. "Why is your side warmer than mine?"

Driver and front seat passenger both get their own heating controls.

So if anyone ever feels chilly, they've only got themselves to blame.

Try turning off the fresh air vent, opening the warm air vent, and redirecting the warm air flow.

(Failing that, try closing the window.)

7. "Have they forgotten the battery?"

As if we'd do a thing like that.

We've merely put it out of harm's way – under the front passenger seat.

It seemed a pity to take up valuable space in either the boot or in the engine compartment.

8. "Where's the spare wheel?"

Obviously, you have to look in the most out-of-the-way places.

But once you know where to find it, it's easy to get at.

Simply lift the floor in the front boot.

9. "Why does it look like a Dinky toy underneath?"

Glad someone asked that question.

We fitted that flat, smooth plate of steel to shut in all the parts that need protecting.

And shut out all the things they need protecting from: dirt, rain, stones and salt.

10. "How can a man in your position afford a car like this?"

Three ways to answer this one:

(a) Admit it only costs £1,470.

(b) Let them go on thinking it costs around £2,000.

(c) Say you've answered enough silly questions for one day.

A force d'être démodé, on finit par être à la mode.

Les années 30 ont vu naître la Coccinelle. Et les robes de nos grand-mères. Mais la jeunesse a le goût du changement.

Les robes de nos grand-mères ont vite passé de mode. Et on a dit la même chose de la Coccinelle.

Pourtant on l'achetait. Tant et si bien qu'il y en a maintenant 13 millions dans le monde.

Et pendant tout ce temps, la philosophie de Volkswagen n'a pas varié : « Bien faire et laisser dire ».

Nous avons laissé dire que le moteur de la Coccinelle n'était pas assez poussé (la mode voulait alors qu'une voiture fasse beaucoup de bruit et qu'elle aille de plus en plus vite).

Et nous avons bien fait. Car c'est pour cette raison que la Coccinelle a un moteur robuste. Et que ceux qui l'achètent apprécient de pouvoir rouler pendant 100 000 km sans connaître de problème.

Nous avons laissé dire que la carrosserie solide de la Coccinelle alourdissait sa ligne, avec ses tôles épaisses, ses grands pare-chocs et ses 8 couches de peinture.

Et nous avons bien fait. Parce que c'est la voiture que les parents préfèrent offrir à leurs enfants. Pour les sentir en sécurité.

Nous avons laissé dire qu'elle avait une ligne rococo et démodée. Avec ses ailes qui débordent, ses gros phares tout ronds et son capot arrondi.

Et là encore nous avons bien fait. Parce que c'est cela qui lui donne un style bien à elle, qui fait que les jeunes la trouvent sympathique et s'y sentent bien.

Au point de s'en servir pour sortir leurs petites amies, pour retrouver leurs copains dans un endroit à la mode. Et pour se distinguer des autres voitures grisâtres qui courent les rues.

Nous avons bien fait de laisser dire tout cela.

Et de penser qu'une voiture solide et robuste sera toujours à la mode.

En un mot, les chiens aboient et la Coccinelle passe.

If he can make it, so can Volkswagen.

No disrespect intended, Mr. Feldman.

But no-one would ever mistake you for Gregory Peck. Yet you've made it right to the top.

On talent.

And that's kind of reassuring when you make a car that looks like ours.

The Volkswagen isn't pretty, Mr. Feldman. But it's got talent.

It has an air-cooled engine that can't boil over in the summer.

Or freeze up in the winter.

It's the kind of engine that can go on and on and on.

We know one person who went right on for 248,000 miles.

And for a little car it's got a great talent for fitting people in.

There's more headroom than you'd expect. (Over 37½" from seat to roof .

If you were 6' 7" Mr. Feldman you still wouldn't hit the roof.

And because there's no engine in the front, there's room to stretch your legs in the front.

We've even got a space behind the back seat where you can sleep a baby.

 In a carrycot.

So you see, Mr. Feldman, looks aren't everything are they?

VOLKSWAGEN MOTORS LIMITED VOLKSWAGEN HOUSE PURLEY SURREY TELEPHONE: 01-668 4100

"The last thing we'd use our camper for is camping."

Amongst our fan mail at Volkswagen we come across a letter telling us what to do with our camper.

Mrs. Felicity Little of Salisbury claims she's used her camper for almost everything. Except camping.

("We've had a VW camper for 5 years and never camped once.")

In fact, so inspired were her uses we thought we'd pass them on.

It should also make it easier for you to part with £2,000 for something you thought you could only use two weeks a year and the occasional weekend.

Charabanc.

"There's less travel sickness due to good vision and less boredom for children who can see over hedges."

The same good vision makes it safer for driving, and especially overtaking."

The new more powerful 1700 engine makes overtaking easier too. And with a top speed of 78 m.p.h., it isn't slow in getting you from A to B.

Nor is the Caravette backward when it comes to seating. All seven seats are forward facing so everybody can see where they're going.

Dining Car.

When you find a spot for lunch, your luxurious limousine transforms into a restaurant.

In a jiff, a working top unhinges to reveal a cooker (two rings and a grill) and stainless steel sink unit.

The other kitchen unit is the cooler. It'll keep cool a welcome cubic foot of beer.

"You can travel without sour milk and your butter won't run away."

Beach Hut.

You'll find our VW a nice change from changing in public.

(It also saves you getting your knickers in a twist whilst trying to hold the towel up at the same time.)

Mrs. Little finds with the beach hut that "Sand sweeps straight out of the doors (and dog hairs) and no carpet to worry about."

She also mentioned another seaside use. That of sailing.

As a chandlery she finds the camper ideal.

The whole most of the dinghy fits neatly inside.

So does all the other sailing equipment. (Including the sailors.)

Removal Van.

"With two adults, four kids (two of them teenagers, two dogs, both labradors), 19" TV, Flymo, cats and basket, hamster and cage," Mrs. Little needs something more than an estate car, yet not quite a van.

"As it's surprisingly just over a foot longer and only 6½" wider than the Beetle" she finds it "easy to drive and handle, and as a woman" she gets "terrific respect from other road users who think it's a big vehicle."

Spare Room.

If you're visited by a large family or if you're a large family visiting, it's useful to have a spare bedroom when the spare bedroom's full.

The Caravette will accommodate four adults. Two up (in the pop-up roof), two down.

If you think you can better Mrs. Little's achievements with a VW camper we'd like to know.

Or for more information about our '74 range fill in the coupon.

You'll receive a brochure and copy of Mrs. Little's letter.

It's a very moving story.

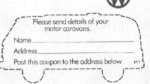

Please send details of your motor caravans.

Name _____

Address _____

Post this coupon to the address below

See the world from the comfort of your own home.

You can go to the ends of the earth in a Volkswagen motor caravan without ever getting homesick.

All the old familiar comforts of home go with you.

You've got your own double bed. (Plus a couple of bunks for the kids.)

You've got a sofa, a dining table, a wardrobe, a cooker, even a kitchen sink.

In fact, as homes go, it's pretty much like any other. Except you can change its address everyday.

And wherever you decide to go, you'll have no trouble getting there.

Up mountains, through snows, across deserts, a VW's an intrepid traveller.

The engine is in the back. It gives the rear wheels much better traction on snow or sand.

Since it's cooled by air too, it never needs water or anti-freeze.

And since it's only as long as a saloon, it's easy to handle and park.

Which makes it a useful car to have around the town.

When you've been around the world.

There goes your holiday for the next few years.

Buying a VW caravan may not leave you much cash for a holiday.

But then, with a VW caravan you don't need much cash for a holiday.

You've booked your seat to wherever you want to go this year.

And you've got your hotel for when you get there.

Because a VW caravan is full of home-from-home comforts.

Beds for two adults and two kids. A cooker. Dining table. Cupboards. Wardrobe. Even a kitchen sink.

And if you want a room overlooking the sea, you can have one.

(It's just a matter of picking your parking spot.)

Of course, once you've got a VW caravan, you're fixed up for next year's holiday too.

And for as many years as you keep your caravan.

But if £1380 still sounds like a lot of holiday money, look at it this way.

What other holiday turns into an estate car as soon as you get home?

Sommes-nous vraiment connus?

1. Connaissez-vous une voiture dont le moteur n'utilise ni eau, ni antigel et qui démarre au 1/4 de tour, même par moins 40°?

OUI	NON

2. Connaissez-vous une voiture qui puisse rouler pendant des heures à 125 km/h sans fatigue pour le moteur?

OUI	NON

3. Connaissez-vous une voiture ayant un moteur de 44 CV/DIN qui fasse 100.000 kilomètres sans problème?

OUI	NON

4. Connaissez-vous une voiture qui a des pare-chocs de 6 cm, et des tôles plus épaisses que celles de ses concurrentes?

OUI	NON

5. Connaissez-vous une voiture ayant un coffre avant dans lequel 260 litres de vin tiennent facilement?

OUI	NON

6. Connaissez-vous une voiture dont la suspension (4 roues indépendantes) soit la même que celle d'une Porsche?

OUI	NON

7. Connaissez-vous une voiture fabriquée depuis 26 ans à plus de 14 millions d'exemplaires et qui soit toujours à la mode?

OUI	NON

8. Connaissez-vous une voiture qui puisse aussi bien être celle d'un PDG, d'un étudiant, d'un médecin ou d'un ecclésiastique?

OUI	NON

9. Enfin, la question subsidiaire (pour vous départager): pourriez-vous dessiner les 2 lettres qui forment notre sigle?

Vous avez 9 oui : Ce n'est pas possible! Vous en possédez une. Félicitations!
Vous avez entre 8 et 6 oui : Cela explique peut-être que vous n'en ayiez pas encore.
Vous avez 5 oui et au-dessous : Nous vous conseillons d'aller très vite chez un concessionnaire
de notre marque. (Il y en a plus de 235 en France).

Doyle Dane Bernbach

A complete list of 1200 c.c. cars that cost less than the Volkswagen 1200.

Skoda Combi Estate.

A complete list of 1300 c.c. cars that cost less than the Volkswagen 1300.

Triumph Herald 13/60.

A complete list of 1500 c.c. cars that cost less than the Volkswagen 1500.

Well done, the both of you.

VOLKSWAGEN MOTORS LIMITED VOLKSWAGEN HOUSE PURLEY SURREY TELEPHONE 01 668 4100

See this unique demonstration at any Volkswagen showroom.

Hello, I'm speaking from the front boot of the Volkswagen 1600 Variant.

My colleague is lying down in the rear boot.

A convincing demonstration, if ever there was one, that the Volkswagen Variant has two boots.

With the back seat down, you can carry objects of up to 5'4" in length.

As you can see, my colleague is 6'2."

However, most children could stretch out comfortably and sleep.

Here in front, there's over 8 cu.ft.of luggage space. So the suitcases and the kids needn't get mixed up.

Where's the engine? I thought you'd never ask.It's tucked away safely under the floor at the back.

And since it's a Volkswagen engine you rarely have to go near it.

In addition, there's a dual-braking system,a cruising speed of over 80 mph and VW service.

And if you've got a little more money there's even a version with electronic fuel injection.

In my opinion, you won't find better value for money anywhere.

And I know my lying colleague would agree.

Les savants prédisent qu'aux environs des années 3000, les insectes auront envahi le monde.

Telle est la loi de la nature : seuls les mieux adaptés survivront.
Et parmi ces insectes, nous savons que les coccinelles seront les mieux adaptés aux conditions de vie des années 3000.
Dans une circulation aussi dense que celle qui est prévue, les coccinelles seront les seules à pouvoir manœuvrer.
La pollution atmosphérique ayant rendu la visibilité très réduite, de nombreux accidents sont à redouter.
Et seules les tôles épaisses des coccinelles

et leurs pare-chocs de 6 cm pourront résister à toutes les mauvaises rencontres.
Le climat, lui, sera devenu extrêmement changeant. Et seules les coccinelles au moteur refroidi par air pourront démarrer par un matin glaciaire, et rouler longtemps sans chauffer pendant une après-midi tropicale.
Quant aux qualités économiques des coccinelles (peu d'entretien, une vidange tous les 5000 km seulement,

ce sont des valeurs qui ne se dévaluent jamais. Nous ne pensons pas que les gens voudront investir plus dans leurs voitures en l'an 3000 qu'en l'an 1971.
Telle est la prédiction des plus éminents savants. Elle prouve que la coccinelle a beau avoir aujourd'hui 35 ans, elle reste la voiture de l'avenir. Et ce n'est pas nous qui irons contre l'avis de la Faculté.

Qui a dit que la Coccinelle était une voiture sans histoires ?

Hier sehen Sie den ersten Wagen von Antarctica.

Dies ist der erste VW im Südpolgebiet. Er ist das erste Fahrzeug in der Antarktis, das nicht speziell für die Antarktis gebaut ist.
Wie Raupenschlepper. Traktoren. Hundeschlitten. R. McMahon, Leiter einer australischen Forschungsgruppe, fährt diesen Wagen.

Über Eis. Durch Schnee. Bei 32 Grad unter Null. Er fährt ihn nicht zum Vergnügen.
Er fährt ihn als Erkundungswagen. Als Begleitfahrzeug für Traktorenzüge. Als Schlepper für Hundeschlitten.
McMahon „Der Wagen fährt, als sei er speziell

für die Antarktis gebaut."
Falls Sie, statt durch die Eiswüste, durch die Wüste fahren wollen.
Wir haben auch einen Wagen, der speziell für die Wüste gebaut zu sein scheint.
Mit Sonnendach.

La nouvelle Coccinelle change de file.

Fini le complexe de la file de droite.
Nous avons donné à la nouvelle Coccinelle 10 CV de plus. Avec 44 CV Din et une vitesse de 135 km/h, elle peut maintenant jouer les chefs de file.
À gauche. Et dans n'importe quelle côte. Avec le plaisir de la vitesse nous lui avons d'ailleurs fait prendre d'autres habitudes.
Par exemple, elle peut avaler d'un

seul coup 260 litres de valises ou de provisions. Nous avons pensé qu'un coffre plus grand ferait plaisir à tout le monde.
Et depuis qu'on a réduit son rayon de braquage à 4,50 m, elle se gare maintenant en 2 coups de volant (c'est quand même plus commode que de pousser devant ou derrière).
Enfin elle a une nouvelle climatisation,

perfectionnée. Avec 9 bouches d'aération et 4 bouches de chauffage (le climat français est tellement changeant). Bien entendu, depuis 25 ans que nous l'améliorons, elle est toujours solide, économique et sûre.
Alors ce n'est pas parce que la nouvelle Coccinelle change de file que nous allons quitter cette voie-là.

It comes in its own garage.

The way we paint a Volkswagen, it's like painting a garage onto it.

First of all, we degrease it. (You don't build a garage on dodgy foundations.)

Then we wash it.

And dip it in phosphate to ward off rust and corrosion.

After that, we wash it.

And after that, we wash it again.

Now for the primer, which we put on in a rather special way:

Electrophoretically.

If you can't pronounce it, no matter. What it means is that you get a more even finish, thicker on the ridges. And no runs.

Next comes the filler coat. And only when that's dry and sanded smooth do we give it the final enamel top coat.

Sprayed on. By hand.

What emerges is a Volkswagen wearing 13lbs of colourful garage:

lbs that'll save you £s later on.

Because with a finish like that, it's less likely to crack up in the frost or wear thin in the rain.

£989 may be a bit steep for a garage. But it's the only one we know that comes with a car under it.

Few things in life work as well as a Volkswagen.

Beetles start from £989 inc.VAT and Car Tax. Delivery, seat belts, number plates extra. Prices may be subject to a currency surcharge. They are immediately available.
VOLKSWAGEN GB LTD, VOLKSWAGEN HOUSE, BRIGHTON ROAD, PURLEY, SURREY. TELEPHONE: 01-668 4100. A MEMBER OF THE THOMAS TILLING GROUP.

It'll pass most other cars on the road. Eventually.

Our 1600cc Super Beetle can't claim to satisfy the Jackie Stewarts of this world. It may be nippier than other Beetles (0-50 mph in 12.5 seconds).

But with a top speed of 81 mph it isn't likely to break any lap records.

However, there are compensations.

Apart from an obvious saving in petrol (Super Beetle averages about 31 mpg) there's a big saving in effort.

While other cars are bursting their boilers at 5,000 revs, Super Beetle cruises flat out all day at 4,000 revs.

Barely enough to work up a sweat let alone work itself to death.

Then, as other cars start to feel their age, Super Beetles still going strong.

It has an oven-baked finish. To make sure its body doesn't crack up before its engine does.

It also has a flat, smooth plate of steel to protect the underside. And keep out all the nasty things that can eat up a car.

In fact, a Super Beetle keeps going so well that you end up overtaking a lot of cars that overtook you.

You might not be going anywhere too quickly.

But isn't that better than getting nowhere fast?

Before you buy a new car, try this simple test.

Take a peek under the car.

It's surprising what you'll see.

Under a Volkswagen, for example, you'll see very little.

No cables. No exposed wires.

Just a flat, smooth plate of steel that completely shuts out the view.

And the dirt, rain, stones and salt that can eventually destroy your car.

While you're down there, take a look at the paintwork, too.

That's right, paintwork.

Even surfaces you can't see, Volkswagen paint like surfaces you can.

Flawlessly.

Before a VW gets the okay to leave the factory, it has to be okayed by 1037 inspectors. If just one of them says No – then No it is!

This might all strike you as an awful lot of trouble to take for a car that costs only £685.

You're right.

You're absolutely right.

You could learn a lot from Mr. Statter.

Every day of the week, Mr Statter hands his car over to some of the worst drivers in the country.

Which is why Mr Statter owns a Volkswagen.

The Volkswagen might have been made for bad drivers.

Its engine is so low-revving it's virtually impossible to over-strain it.

One VW owner (we have the name and address) actually got 248,000 miles from a single engine.

So a heavy-footed learner isn't going to break it.

The VW gearbox can stand a little clutch-less gear changing, now and again.

Even though there's a clutch.

And when someone drives Mr Statters car into a gatepost, it isn't going to drive him out of business.

We can fit a new wing in just one hour.

10 bolts off, 10 bolts on. (With most cars the whole side has to come out.)

All told, some 55 driving schools in the UK use Volkswagens.

And if they can stand up to all those bad drivers, they can certainly stand up to you.

Wait till she finds out it's only a Volkswagen.

It's easy for a poor, unsuspecting girl to be taken in by your VW Fastback.

To all appearances, it's a racy foreign G.T. owned by some wealthy gadabout.

She's not to know it's really a solid, dependable sort of car owned by a solid, dependable sort of fellow.

And maybe you'd better not tell her.

She might be disappointed to learn that it costs a paltry £1,114.

That it scrimps and saves on petrol. (Gets nearly 30 mpg.)

That you rarely dip into your pocket for repairs and tune-ups.

And that you aren't planning to swap it for the next fashionable sports job that comes along. Because, being a VW, it's built to last.

Of course, if you feel like pushing your luck, go ahead and put her straight.

If she doesn't walk out on you, congratulations.

It isn't your money she's after.

It's you.

Si tout était à recommencer, il ne faudrait pas oublier les Coccinelles.

Irrité de la conduite des hommes, Dieu décida de leur infliger à nouveau le châtiment du déluge. Dieu dit à Noé : «Tu prendras deux de chaque espèce, et tu n'oublieras pas les coccinelles».

Et Noé dit : «Sont-elles bien nécessaires?»

Dieu, courroucé, répondit : «La coccinelle est l'amie de l'homme. Elle a la solidité de la tortue, la sobriété du chameau, la longévité de l'éléphant».

Alors Noé regarda la coccinelle. Et il vit sa carapace en tôle épaisse, recouverte de sept couches de peinture et protégée par de gros pare-chocs.

Puis Noé regarda le moteur. Et il vit qu'il n'utilisait pas d'eau parce qu'il était refroidi par air. Il vit sa robustesse, qui permettait à la coccinelle de rouler 100 000 km sans problèmes.

Noé vit aussi qu'elle était si facile à

manœuvrer qu'il pourrait la ranger n'importe où dans son arche. Et Noé sut que le Seigneur avait raison.

L'Eternel vit que Noé obéissait à son commandement, et il dit :

 «Tu ne le regretteras point, car la postérité des petites bêtes à Bon Dieu sera une bénédiction pour l'humanité».

Et Noé loua le Seigneur.

Which way does your money go?

Most cars can only lead you in one direction. On the road to ruin.

But not so a Volkswagen.

While other cars are busy eating up the petrol, a VW is busy eating up the miles. (100,000 miles on the clock is far from a freak).

In fact, it's where other cars fade that a VW shines.

Park it out in the rain and it flourishes. (There's 13 lbs. of paint that come between you and a bill).

Unfortunately, another example isn't so shining:

The underneath.

Take a peak and all you'll see is a flat, smooth plate of steel that shuts out the view.

And the dirt, rain, stones and salt that eventually destroy your car.

When the day of reckoning comes, when you finally decide to part company with your Volkswagen, it won't break your heart.

Unlike so many cars, a VW doesn't depreciate wildly as soon as you turn the ignition. Which all adds up to you getting a tidy price for your Volkswagen.

You can bank on it.

They are still two of the cheapest ways of crossing the country.

This is a timely reminder from VW that a Beetle can do 38 miles to a gallon of 3 star.

40,000 miles to a set of tyres. Often 100,000 to an engine. That it never needs anti-freeze. Hardly ever needs oil. And holds its value like few others in Glass's Guide.

So that even at £989 for a basic model, a Beetle's a bargain.

So is a new 3½p stamp, if it's used properly.

If you stick one on an envelope and address it to Volkswagen (GB) Ltd., Volkswagen House, Purley, Surrey we'll send you a Beetle brochure.

Absolutely free.

Few things in life work as well as a Volkswagen.

Recommended price VW 1200 L saloon, VAT and Car Tax £989 only as at ... ... prices to change without notice subject to hire purchase offer 1974.
VOLKSWAGEN (GB) LTD. VOLKSWAGEN HOUSE, BRIGHTON ROAD, PURLEY, SURREY. TELEPHONE ... ... A MEMBER OF THE THOMAS TILLING GROUP.

We've made so many improvements they're beginning to show.

At first glance, our new 1303 Beetle looks much the same as any other Beetle.

But we have to tell you, it's a changed car.

Take another look at the windscreen.

It's 42% bigger and curved.

From a 1303 you can see a lot more of the world around you.

Of course, we believe that being seen in a 1303 is just as important as being able to see out.

That's why we've made the rear lights as big as headlights.

They actually measure 6½ inches across.

The bumper, we've moved a bit further out from the body, since we understand 'touch' parking is on the increase.

As far as the engine went, we couldn't make it go much further.

So we settled for making you the offer of one that goes faster.

The standard 1303 has a 1300cc Beetle engine; the 1303S has a 1600cc Beetle engine.

Inside, we've really had a ball.

The first thing you won't recognise is the dash.

It's padded, covered in black anti-glare material and fitted with rocker switches.

On top of that, the speedometer is set in an anti-dazzle cowling.

Just like you get on expensive cars.

The seats have a new feel to them too.

They're contoured to accommodate every curve of your body. Or anyone else's.

And the front seats adjust to 77 positions.

Find the right position and you'll find long journeys a lot less tiring.

Lift the bonnet of a 1303 and you're in for another surprise.

The boot is 80% bigger than the boot of the standard 1300.

Because a different kind of suspension up front absorbs the bumps without absorbing so much luggage space.

In some ways, of course, a new Beetle is no different from an old Beetle.

It's just as reliable, economical and lasts just as long.

The new 1303 Beetle.

Going, going...

So finally the time has come.

The Beetle is about to bid adieu.

For nearly a quarter of a century, it's been a faithful friend.

In all that time, it never set much store by the way it looked.

Only by the way it worked.

It revived the honesty of words like economical.

And reliable. And durable.

With the Beetle, you could believe them.

A lot of people did. More than 19 million altogether.

If you want to join them, you'll have to move fast.

Because the very last of the Beetles have already been brought into the country.

Chin up, though.

Knowing how long Beetles last, it'll be a long time before you've seen the last of them.

The New Beetle.

In January 1994 Volkswagen of America stunned the automotive world with Concept 1.

A new car with an unmistakably familiar shape.It was instantly dubbed the New Beetle.

Initially conceived as little more than a design exercise, public demand encouraged VW to put the car into production.

The US advertising created by Boston based Arnold Communications won praise and prizes the world over.

The UK advertising from DDB's London office looks set to follow suit.

If you were really good in a past life,
you come back as something better.

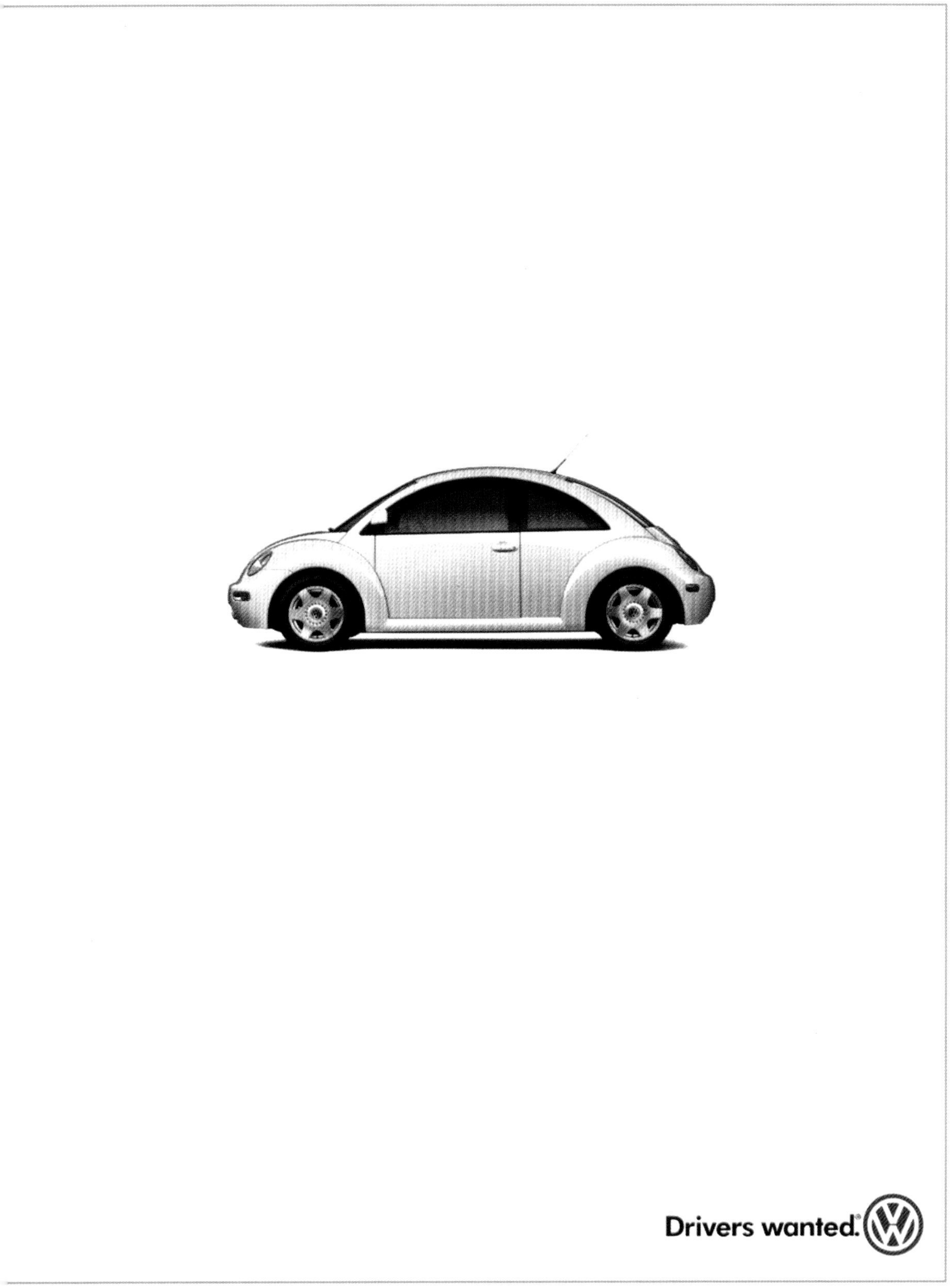
Drivers wanted.®

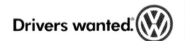

The engine's in the front,
but its heart's in the same place.

Drivers wanted.

Is it possible to go backwards and
forwards at the same time?

Drivers wanted.

A car like this comes around
only twice in a lifetime.

Drivers wanted.

Digitally remastered.

Drivers wanted.

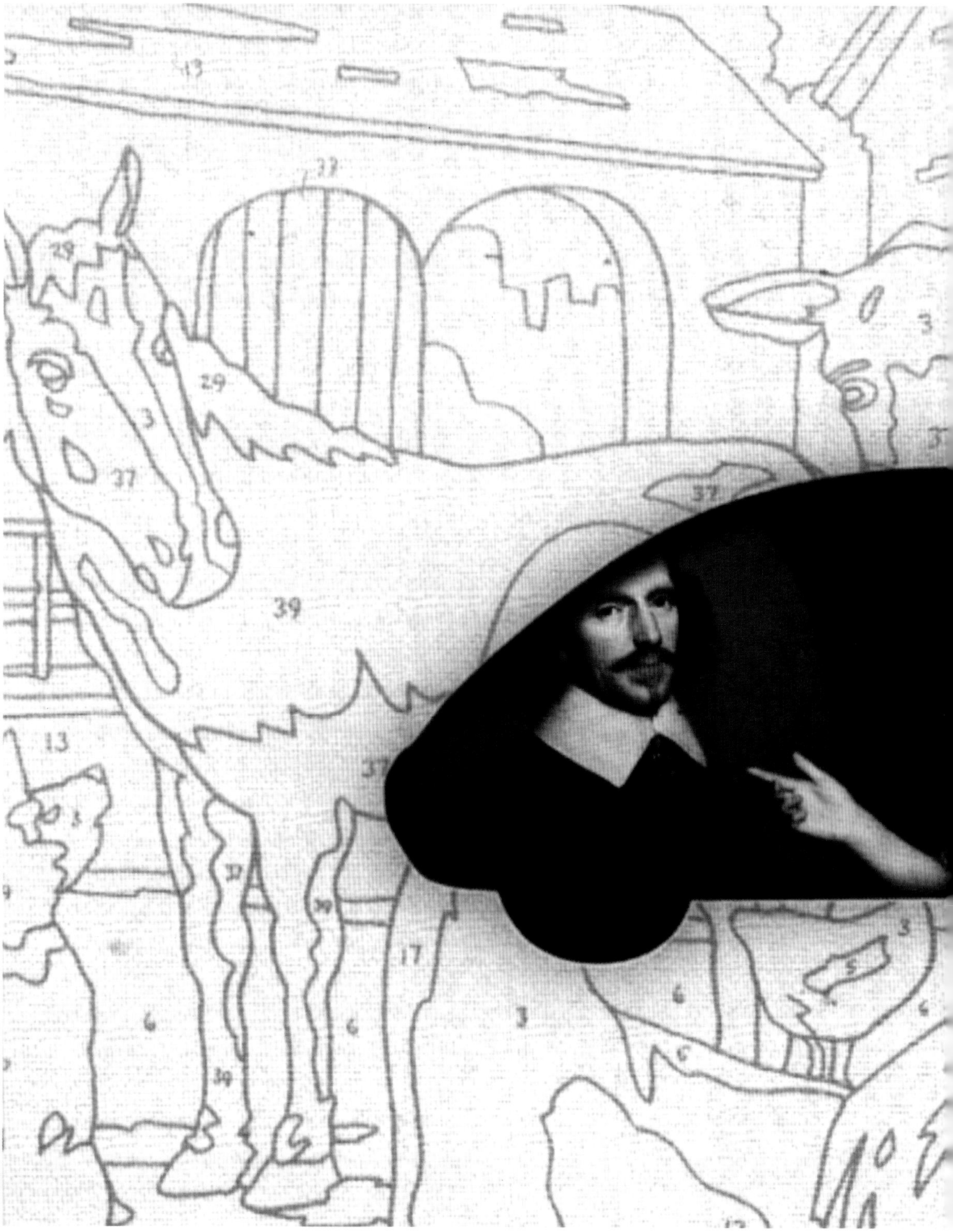

The new Beetle. Fun on the outside, serious underneath

2.0 litre, 115 bhp, electronic stability programme. £14,950 rrp

The new Beetle. Fun on the outside, serious underneath
2.0 litre, 115 bhp, electronic stability programme. £14,950 rrp

The new Beetle. Fun on the outside, serious underneath
2.0 litre, 115 bhp, electronic stability programme. £14,950 rrp